# Design and Analysis of Algorithms

Dr.P. Sudhakar

M. Gunasekar

V. Kavitha

**Published by**

BONFRING®
Intellectual Integrity

**Design and Analysis of Algorithms**



ISBN 978-93-86176-29-5

**Authors**

Dr.P. Sudhakar

M. Gunasekar

V. Kavitha

**Bonfring**

309, 2nd Floor, 5th Street Extension, Gandhipuram,

Coimbatore-641 012.

Tamilnadu, India.

E-mail: info@bonfring.org

Website: www.bonfring.org

Phone: 0422 4213231

# Preface

Design and Analysis of Algorithms is the one of the fundamental concept in the field of both computing science. This text book enables the users to understand the fundamental concepts of algorithm design. This book is written as a text book for the students of computer science, information technology & computing applications.

We have designed this book to make students easily understand the concepts and features of Algorithm design to share with you the knowledge about how to develop Algorithms. We hope that by helping you to understand the fundamentals of Algorithms and problem solving strategy, you will be equipped to face all the challenges in developing a program.

We have given importance to the different Algorithm design techniques and to Algorithm analysis. We have given attention to some of the important design techniques which are currently used in practice to solve complex problems. We also hope to serve the programming community at large to build solutions for complex problems.

## Features

1. To understand the principle of Algorithm design techniques.

2. To learn how to solve the complex problems.

3. To learn about some of the key aspect of Algorithm design techniques.

4. To analyze the efficiency of the Algorithm with respect to space and time complexity.

*Dr.P. Sudhakar*

*M. Gunasekar*

*V. Kavitha*

# Acknowledgement

I am very grateful to **Shri.M.Kumarasamy**, Founder and Honorable Chairman of the renowned institution M.Kumarasamy College of Engineering, Karur for his moral support to bring out this book.

I express my sincere thanks to Respected Secretary **Dr.K.Ramakrishnan** and Trustee Madam Smt.Vijaya Ramakrishnan of M.Kumarasamy College of Engineering, Karur for their constant support.

My heart is filled with happiness to thank **Dr.V.Kavitha**, Principal of M.Kumarasamy College of Engineering, Karur for their unstinted support and guidance. Heartful gratitude to **Dr.S.Kuppusamy**, Executive Director, M.Kumarasamy College of Engineering, Karur for providing encouragement at all times.

I am especially grateful to **Bonfring Publications** who have shown keen interest in publishing this book.

I dedicate this book to my dear better half **Mrs.P.Sathya B.E.,** who encourages me towards all my endeavors.

*Dr.P. Sudhakar*

I dedicate this book to My father **Mr.T.Manickasundaram** & My mother **Mrs.T.Sampooranam** who brought me into the world & My better half **Mrs.K.Sangeetha** who brought all success in my life and I thank all my friends, relatives, colleagues for theirs continuous support & blessings.

*M. Gunasekar*

I dedicate this book to My father **Mr.A.K.Velusamy** & My mother **V.Jothimani** who brought me into the world & My dear better half **Mr.R. Rameshprabhu** who brought all success in my life and I thank all my friends,relatives,colleagues for theirs continuous support & blessings.

*V. Kavitha*

# Author's Profile

**Dr.P. Sudhakar** received his Masters in Technology-Computer Science and Engineering from SRM University. He had received his PhD in the field of Network Security from PRIST University. He has participated in more than 20 national & international level conferences around the world. He has published more than 13+ papers in various reputed journals. He has published two text books in the name of Mobile Computing An extensive analysis, Computer Networking a simple learning. He has received *"Young Scientist Award–2015"* by Venus International Foundation" for his untired research effort & *"Best Administrator Award–2015"* by ASDF. He is having more than 10 years experience in academics. Now presently he is working as Professor&Head of Information Technology in M.Kumarasamy College of Engineering, Karur.

**M. Gunasekar** received his Bachelors of Technology in Information Technology and Masters of Engineering in Computer Science Engineering from Anna University Chennai. He has presented papers in various National and International conferences. He is having 4.5 years of experience in academics. At present he is working as Assistant Professor in the department of Information Technology in M.Kumarasamy College of Engineering, Karur. His area of interest is Data Structures and Computer Networks.

**V. Kavitha** received her Bachelor's of Engineering in Computer Science Engineering from VLB Janakiammal College of Engineering and Technology & Masters of Engineering-Computer Science and Engineering from M.Kumarasamy College of Engineering Karur. She has presented papers on more than 8 National & International level conferences. She has published 5 papers in various reputed journals. She is having 9.3 Years of Experience in academics. Now presently she is working as Assistant Professor-Computer Science Engineering in M.Kumarasamy College of Engineering Karur. Her area of interest is Object Oriented concepts and Problem solving Techniques.

<table>
<tr><td>Unit</td><td style="text-align:center">Contents</td><td>Page No</td></tr>
</table>

# UNIT 1

## Basic Concepts of Algorithms

Basic Concepts – Notion of Algorithm – Fundamentals of Algorithmic Solving – Important Problem types – Fundamentals of Analysis Framework – Asymptotic Notations and Basic Efficiency Classes. Mathematical Analysis of Non–recursive Algorithm – Mathematical Analysis of Recursive Algorithm.

## 1.  Analysis of Algorithms

## 1.1. Algorithm Analysis

### *Algorithm*

- An Algorithm is a finite set of instructions that if followed, accomplishes a particular task.

- An algorithm is the actual procedure to solve a particular problem, which can be easily understood by any solution provider or any programmer who is going to implement the solution.

- An algorithm is step by step procedure to solve a problem.

### *1.1.1.  Notation of Algorithm*

- An algorithm is a sequence of non ambiguous instructions for solving problem in a finite amount of time.

- An input to an algorithm specifies an instance of the problem.

- An algorithm can be specified in a natural language or a pseudo code.

- Algorithm can be implemented as computer programs.

- An algorithm is a sequence of finite number of steps involved in solving a problem.

- Each algorithm is a module, designed to handle specific problem relative to particular data Structure.

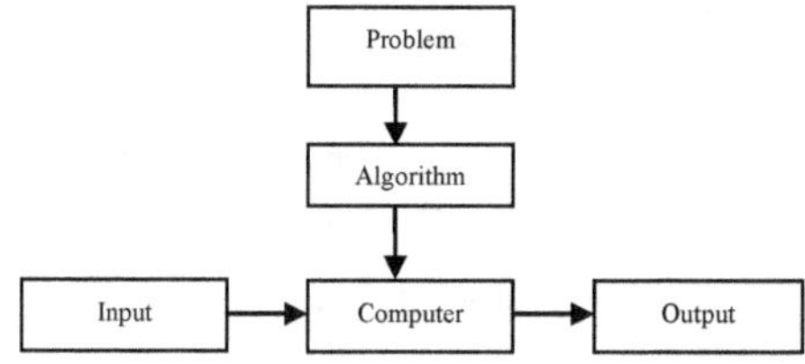


Fig. 1.1: Notation of Algorithm

Algorithms that are definite and effective are also called **computational procedures**. A **Program** is the expression of an algorithm in a programming language.

## *Characteristics of an Algorithm*

The important and prime characteristics of an algorithm are

### 1.  *Input*

Zero (or) more quantities externally supplied

### 2.  *Output*

At least one quantity is produced.

### 3.  *Definiteness*

Each instruction is clear and ambiguous.

### 4.  *Finiteness*

It we trace out the instruction of an algorithm then for all cases, the algorithm terminates after a finite number of steps.

### 5.  *Efficiency*

Every instruction must be very basic so that it can be carried out in principle  by a person using pencil and paper.

### 6.  *Unambiguity*

An algorithm must be expressed in a fashion that is completely free of ambiguity.

### *1.1.2.  Study of Algorithm*

The study of algorithm involves 3 major parts.

1.  Designing the algorithm
2.  Proving the correctness of the algorithm
3.  Analyzing the algorithm.

### 1.  *Designing the Algorithm*

- It is a method for solving a problem.
- Each step of an algorithm must be precisely defined and no vague statements should be used.
- Pseudo code is used to describe the algorithm.

## 2. Proving the Correctness of the Algorithm

- We have to prove that the algorithm yields a required result for every Legitimate input in a finite amount of time.
- A human must be able to perform each step using pencil and paper by giving the required input, use the algorithm and should get the required output in a finite amount of time.

## 3. Analyzing the Algorithms

- It deals with the amount of time and space consumed by it.
- Efficient algorithm can be computed with minimum requirement of time and space.
- Time and space complexity can be reduced only to certain levels.

### 1.1.3. The Need for Algorithm Analysis

The following criteria used to identify the best algorithm.

## Criteria

### 1. Time Efficiency

The time required to run for an algorithm

### 2. Space Efficiency

The space need for an algorithm

### 3. Measuring an Input's Size

The algorithm efficiency depends on input size.

Almost all algorithm run longer on larger inputs.

Example: Computing the product of two n-by-n matrices.

### 4. Units for Measuring Running Time

Some units of time measurement such as a second, a millisecond and so on can be used to measure the running time of a program implementing the algorithm.

Example: Most sorting algorithms work by comparing elements of a list being sorted with each other.

For such algorithms, the basic operation is a key comparison.

## 5. Order of Growth

A difference in running times on small inputs is not what really distinguishes efficient algorithms from inefficient ones.

A few functions particularly important for analysis of algorithms are

| $n$ | $\log_2 n$ | $n$ | $n \log_2 n$ | $n^2$ | $n^3$ | $2^n$ | $n!$ |
|---|---|---|---|---|---|---|---|
| 10 | 3.3 | $10^1$ | $3.3.10^1$ | $10^2$ | $10^3$ | $10^3$ | $3.6.10^6$ |
| $10^2$ | 6.6 | $10^2$ | $6.6.\,10^2$ | $10^4$ | $10^6$ | $1.3.10^{30}$ | $9.3.10^{157}$ |
| $10^3$ | 10 | $10^3$ | $10.\,10^3$ | $10^6$ | $10^9$ | | |
| $10^4$ | 13 | $10^4$ | $13.\,10^4$ | $10^8$ | $10^{12}$ | | |

The efficiencies of some algorithms may differ significantly for inputs of the same size. For such algorithms, we need to distinguish between the Worst case, best case and average case efficiencies.

The framework's primary interest lies in the order of growth of the algorithm's running time? (extra memory units consumed)as its input size goes to infinity.

## 6. Worst Case, Best Case and Average Case Efficiencies

- The worst-case efficiency of an algorithm is its efficiency for the worst case input of size n, which is an input of size n for which the algorithm runs the longest among all possible inputs.
- The best-case efficiency of an algorithm is its efficiency for the worst case input of size n, which is an input of size n for which the algorithm runs the fastest among all possible inputs.
- The Average case efficiency of an algorithm is its efficiency for the random input of size n, which makes some assumptions about possible inputs of size n.

### 1.1.4. Example — Multiply 2 integer numbers. This example explains now one algorithm may be superior to others in terms of computation time or memory space.

- A problem may be solved by different methods resulting in the some solution.
- Here we take the multiplication of 2 positive integers as problem instance.
- 3 different methods are used to solve this problem.

## *Method 1*

- Usual way of multiplying 2 numbers

## *Example*

```
25X12
50
25
300
```

## *Method 2*

- This method is known as ala russe.
- The 2 numbers are written in 2 columns.
- Each time the smaller number is multiplied by 2 and the large number is divided by 2.
- Take only the integral part of the result in the division.
- Finally see the larger number column, find the rows which have odd values  choose the corresponding number from the smaller number column and place  them in a 3rd column.
- The result is obtained by summing the values in the 3rd column

Example 25 x 12

```
25 12   12
12 24   -
 6  48  -
 3  96  96
 1 192 192
        300
```

- Column I contain 25, 3, 1 these 3 odd numbers.
- The corresponding 12, 96, 192 placed in 3rd column.

## *Method 3*

- This method is known as "Nikilan Navatas caramam Dasatah"
- Take the base near to any multiples of 10.
- In the example of(25 x 12).20 is base.
- We write the first 2 line 20 + 5 = 25, 20- 8 = 12
- The left side of the 3rd line in due to 25 - 8 (or) 12 + 5. (ie) this is performed by across on the first 2 lines.

- The right side is obtained form (+5) x (-8) = - 40.
- Since the 2 first 2 line have one digit to the right by the operators. so -0 is place on the top and the -4, which is the balance is placed slightly below.
- The base 20 i.e., 10 x2 = 20. We multiply the left by 2 which yields 34. Now the balance -4 added with this value. Which implies - 30.
- This value has to the multiplied by 10 as the right side has only one digit.
- The result has to be added with the right side value -0.
- The resultant value would be the required one

$$25+5$$
$$12-8$$

$$17\,|\,-4°$$
$$X$$
$$2$$
$$34\,|\,-4°$$
$$= (34—4)10^-$$
$$=30|\ 0^-$$
$$= (30 \times 10)-0$$
$$=300$$

- Among 3 methods we can use alarusse method to multiply 2 positive integers.
- It requires less time when comparing with method I.
- It is simpler than method 3.

## 1.2. Fundamentals of Algorithmic Problem Solving

A sequence of steps involved in designing and analyzing an algorithm is shown in fig 1.2. The various steps involved in the algorithm design and analysis process are:

1. *Understanding the problem.*
2. *Ascertaining the capabilities of a computational device.*
3. *Choosing between exact and approximate problem solving.*
4. *Deciding an appropriate data structures.*
5. *Algorithm design techniques.*
6. *Methods of specifying an algorithm.*
7. *Proving an algorithm's correctness.*
8. *Analyzing an algorithm.*
9. *Coding an algorithm.*

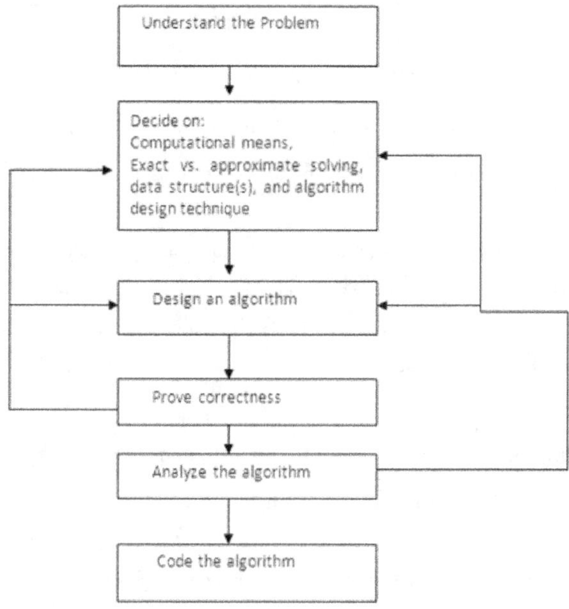



Fig. 1.2: Algorithm Design and Analysis Process

The algorithms are analyzed, with the intention of improving them. The following criteria are used to analyze the algorithm.

1. *Correctness.*
2. *Amount of work done.*
3. *Amount of space used.*
4. *Simplicity.*
5. *Clarity.*
6. *Optimality.*

### 1.2.1. *Understanding the Problem*

- To design an algorithm, understand the problem completely by reading the problem's description carefully.
- If any doubts about the given problem statement, then ask questions to clarify the doubts.
- Do some examples and then think about special cases, if required again ask questions.

- Once the problem is clearly understand, then determine the overall goals, but it should be in a precise manner.
- Then divide the problem into smaller problems until they become manageable size.

### 1.2.2. Ascertaining the Capabilities of a Computational Device

- In random access machine, instruction to be executed one after another, one operation at a time.
- Algorithms designed to be executed on such machines are called sequential algorithms.
- The central assumption of the RAM model does not called for some new computers that can execute operations concurrently (i.e) operations executed in parallel.
- Algorithms that take the advantage of operations that executed concurrently are called parallel algorithms.

### 1.2.3. Choosing Between Exact and Appropriate Problem Solving

- The next principal decision is to choose between solving the problem exactly or solving the problem approximately.
- The algorithm used to solve the problem exactly is called **exact algorithm.**
- The algorithm used to solve the problem approximately is called **approximate algorithm**.

### Reason to Choose Approximate Algorithm

1. There are important problems that simply cannot be solved exactly such as,
   - Extracting square roots.
   - Solving nonlinear equations
   - Evaluating define integrals
2. Available algorithms for solving problem exactly can be unacceptably slow, because of the problem's intrinsic complexity. The well known example is, **travelling salesman problem** of finding the shortest path through n cities.
3. An approximation algorithm can be part of a more sophisticated algorithm that solves a problem exactly.

### 1.2.4. Deciding On Appropriate Data Structures

> Algorithm + data structure=Programs

In object oriented programming, the data structure is important for both design and analysis of algorithms.

Some algorithms do not demand any ingenuity in representing their input but others are predicated on ingenious data structure.

The variability in algorithm is due to in which the data of the program are stored. That is,

- How they are arranged in relation to each other.
- Which data are kept in memory
- Which are kept in files and how the files are arranged
- Which are calculated when needed

### 1.2.5. *Algorithm Design Techniques*

An algorithm design techniques or strategy or paradigm is general approach to solving problems algorithmically that is applicable to a variety of problems from different areas of computing.

### *Uses*

- They provide guidance for designing algorithms foe new problems. (i.e) they provide guidance to problem which has no known satisfied algorithms.
- Algorithm are the cornerstone of computer science.
- Algorithm design techniques is used to classify the algorithms based on the design idea.
- Algorithm design techniques can serve as a natural way to categorize and study the algorithms.

### 1.2.6. *Methods of Specifying an Algorithm*

There are two options, which are widely used to specify the algorithms. They are:

1. *Euclid's algorithm*
2. *Pseudo code*

A pseudo code is a mixture of a natural language and programming language constructs.

A pseudo code is more precise than a natural language.

For simplicity, declaration of the variables is omitted.

For, if and while statements are used to show the scope of the variables.

"←" (Arrow)-used for the assignment operation.

"∕" (two slashes) –used for comments.

In the earlier days of computing, the dominant vehicle for specifying algorithm is flow chart.

### Flow Chart

- It is method of expressing an algorithm by a collection of connected geometric shapes containing description of the algorithms steps.
- It very simple algorithm.

This representation technique is inconvenient.

### 1.2.7. Proving an Algorithm's Correctness

Once an algorithm has been specified, then its correctness must be proved.

That is, the algorithm must yields a required result for every legitimate input in a finite amount of time.

For example, correctness of Euclid's algorithm for computing the Greatest Common Divisor stems from correctness of the equality.

$$Gcd\ (m,n)=gcd\ (n,m,m\ mod\ n)$$

A mathematical induction is a common technique used to prove the correctness of the algorithm.

In mathematical induction, an algorithm's iterations provide a natural sequence of steps needed for proofs.

The notation of correctness for approximation algorithms is less straight forward than it is exact algorithms.

### 1.2.8. Analyzing an Algorithm

Efficiency of an algorithm can be determined by measuring the time, space and amount of resources, it uses for executing the program.

The amount of time taken by an algorithm can be calculated by finding the number of steps the algorithm executes.

The space refers to the number of units it requires for memory storage.

The complexity of an algorithm is measured by calculating the time taken, space required for performing the algorithm.

The efficiency of the algorithm is determined with respect to cntral processing units time and internal memory.

There are two types of algorithm efficiency. They are,

- Time efficiency (or) Time complexity
- Space efficiency (or) Space complexity

### Time Efficiency

Time efficiency indicates how fast the algorithm runs.

If the performance behavior of an algorithm is characterized using the factor, the time taken to solve a problem is known as Time Complexity.

The time taken by a program to complete its task depends on the number of steps in an algorithm.

The time required by a program to complete its task will not always be the same.

It depends on the type of problem to be solved.

It can be comprised of two types.

- *Compilation time*
- *Run Time (or) Execution Time*

The time (T) taken by an algorithm (a) is the sum of the compile time and the execution time.

### Compilation Time

The amount of time taken by the compiler to compile an algorithm is known as compilation time.

During compilation time, it does not calculate the executable statements it calculates only the declaration statements and check for any syntax and semantic errors.

The different compilers can take different times to compile the same program.

### Execution Time

The execution time depends on the size of the algorithm.

If the number of instructions in an algorithm is large then the run time is also large.

The number of instructions in an algorithm is small then the time needed to execute the program is small.

The execution time is calculated for executable statements and not for the declaration statements.

The complexity is normally expressed as an order of magnitude.

Example: $O(n^2)$

The time complexity of a given algorithm is defined as computation of function f () as a total number of statements that are executed for computing the value f(n).

The time complexity is a function which depends on the value of n.

The time complexity can be classified as 3 types. They are:

1. *Worst case analysis*
2. *Average case analysis.*
3. *Best case analysis.*

## *Worst case Analysis*

The worst case complexity for a given size corresponds to the maximum complexity encountered among all problem of the same size.

Worst case complexity takes a longer time to produce a desired result.

This can be represented by a function f(n)

$$F(n) = n^2 \text{ or } n \log n$$

## *Average Case Analysis*

The average case analysis is also known as the **expected complexity** which gives a measure of the behaviour of the algorithm averaged over all possible problem of the same size.

Average case is the time taken by an algorithm for producing a desired output.

## *Best Case Analysis*

Best case is the shortest time taken by an algorithm for producing a desired result.

## *Space Complexity*

Space efficiency indicates how much extra memory the algorithm needs.

During execution the amount of memory consumed by the algorithm is known as space complexity.

The amount of storage space taken by the algorithm depends on the type of the problem to be solved.

The space can be calculated as

1. A fixed amount of memory occupied by the space for the program code is space occupied by the variable used in the program.
2. A variable amount of memory occupied by the component variable, where size is dependent on the problem being solved.

This space is more or less depending upon whether the program uses iterative or recursive procedures.

There are three different space considered for determining the amount of memory used by the algorithm. They are

- *Instruction Space*
- *Data Space*
- *Environment Space*

### Instruction Space

When the program gets compiled, then the space needed to store the complied instruction in the memory is called instruction space.

The instruction space independent of the size of the problem.

### Data Space

The memory space used to hold the variables of data structures and other data elements are called data space.

The data space is related to the size of the problem.

### Environment Space

It is the space in memory used only on the execution time for each function call. It maintains runtime stack in that it holds returning address of the previous functions.

Every function on the stack has return value and a pointer on it.

### Calculation of Space Complexity

The memory space occupied by the various data type is as follow.

- *Character Takes One Unit Of Memory Space.*
- *Integer Takes 2 Units Of Memory Space.*
- *Float Takes Four Units Of Memory Space.*
- *Double Takes Eight Units Of Memory Space.*

For example, consider a code,

```
function()
{
char a[15]
float f
int i
double d
............
............
}
```

The amount of units occupied by each variables

a=25 units

f=4 units

i=2 units

d=8 units

Total number of units =39 units

Space complexity is normally expressed as an order of magnitude.

Example: **$O(n^2)$**

## *Characteristics of Algorithms*

1. *Simplicity*
2. *Generality*

## *Simplicity*

1. Simpler algorithms are easier to understand.
2. Simpler algorithms are easier to program.
3. The resulting programs contains only few bugs.
4. Simpler algorithms are more efficient compared to the complicated alternatives.

### *Generality*

The characteristics of an algorithm generality have two issues.

They are

1.  Generality of the problem the algorithm solves.
2.  Range of inputs it accepts.

### *1.2.9.  Coding an Algorithm*

Implementing an algorithm correctly is necessary but not sufficient to dimnish the algorithm's power by an inefficient implementation.

Modern compilers provide a certain safety net in this regard, especially, when they are used their code optimization mode.

The standard tricks such as computing a loop's invariant (an expression that does not change its value) outside the loop, collecting common sub expressions, replacing expensive operations by cheaper ones and so on should be known to the programmers such factors can speed up a program only by a constant factor, whereas a better algorithm can make a difference in running time by orders of magnitude.

Once an algorithm has been selected, a 10-50% speed up may be worth an effort.

An algorithm's optimality is not about the efficiency of an algorithm but about the complexity of the problem it solves.

Another important issue of algorithmic problem solving is the question of whether or not every problem can be solved by an algorithm.

## 1.3. Important Problem Types

Some of the most important problem types are:

1.  Sorting
2.  Searching
3.  String Matching
4.  Graph Problems
5.  Combinational Problems
6.  Geometric Problems
7.  Numerical Problems

### 1.3.1. *Sorting*

Sorting is an important operations performed most commonly on large storage of information.

In general, sorting is performed in business data processing application and specific application in order to retrieve the information more efficiently.

The process of ordering (or) arranging the quantities (or) given data items in an ascending order or descending order according to some linear relationship among the given data items is known as sorting.

Many algorithms are used to perform the task of sorting.

Sorting is the operation of arranging the records of a table according to the key value of the each record.

A table of a file is an ordered sequence of records r[1],r[2],...r[n] each containing a key k[1],k[2],...,k[n]. The table is sorted based on the key.

### *Properties of Sorting Algorithms*

The two properties of sorting algorithms are

1. Stable
2. In space

A strong algorithm is called stable, if ti preserves the relative order of any two equal elements in its output.

In other words, if an input list contain two equal elements in positions k and l, where  k< l, then in the sorted list they have to be in position k and 'l' respectively, such that  k< l

This property is desirable. For example, to start a list of students in alphabetical order, the sorting is performed according to the student GPA.A stable algorithm will yield a list in which students with the same GPA will still be sorted alphabetically.

The second feature of a sorting algorithm is the amount of extra memory the algorithm requires. An algorithm is said to be in place if it does not require extra memory, except, possibly for a few memory units. The important criteria for the selection of a sorting method for the given set of data items are as follows.

1. Programming Time of the Sorting Algorithm
2. Execution Time of the Program

3. Memory Space Needed for the Programming Environment

The main objectives involved in the design of sorting algorithms are

1. Minimum Number of Exchanges
2. Large Volume of Data Block Environment

Hence the designed and desired sorting algorithm must employ minimum number of exchanges and the data should be moved in large blocks, which in turn increase the efficiency of the sorting algorithm.

## Types of Sorting

The two major classification of sorting methods are

1. Internal Sorting Methods
2. External Sorting Methods

## Internal Sorting Method

The key principle of internal sorting is that all the data items to be sorted are retained in the main memory and random access into this memory space can be effectively used to sort the data items.

## The Various Internal Sorting Methods are

1. Bubble Sort
2. Selection Sort
3. Shell Sort
4. Insertion Sort
5. Quick Sort
6. Heap Sort

## External Sorting

The idea behind the external sorting is to m one data from secondary storage to main memory in large blocks for ordering the data. The most commonly used external sorting method is merge sort.

### 1.3.2. Searching

One of the important applications of array is searching.

Classification:

The searching techniques are classified into two types.

They are

1. Quantity-Dependent Search Techniques
2. Density- Dependent Search Techniques

### *Quantity-Dependent Search Techniques*

The efficiency of quantity dependent search techniques depends on the quantity of records in the list of data items to be searched.

The different types of quantity dependent search techniques are

1. Linear Search Or Sequential Search
2. Binary Search
3. Binary Tree Search

### *Sequential Search*

Sequential search technique is a straight forward technique.

This technique is used when records are not stored in order.

This technique is used when the storage medium locks direct access facilities.

In this technique, search operation is very simple and takes a long time if the array size is large.

The algorithm starts its search with the first available record and proceeds to the next available record repeatedly, until the required data item to be searched is found.

### *Binary Search*

The efficiency of the search effort can be increased by using the simple technique called binary search.

In this technique the data items in the list are stored in alphabetically or numerically increasing order.

The binary search begins in the middle of the list of data items and determines, whether the data item to be searched is available in lower or upper bound of the list and then continues the process of divided that portion of the list, till the item to be searched is located.

The method requires less number of comparisons than sequential search to locate the given data.

### *1.3.3.  String Processing*

A string is a sequence of characters from an alphabet.

Different types of strings are

1.  Text String
2.  Bit String

### *Text String*

It is a collection of letters, numbers and special characters.

### *Bit String*

It is a collection of zeros and ones

### *Gene Sequence*

It can be modeled by strings of characters from the four character alphabet {A,C.G,T}

The different operations performed on a string are

1.  Reading and Writing String
2.  String Concatenation
3.  Finding String Length
4.  String Copy
5.  String Comparison
6.  Substring Operations
7.  Insertion into a String
8.  Deletions from A String
9.  Pattern Matching

### *Pattern Matching or String matching*

The process of searching for an occurrence of word in a text is called pattern matching.

Some of the algorithms used for pattern matching are:

1.  Simple Pattern Matching
2.  Pattern Matching Using Morris Prat Algorithm
3.  Pattern Matching Using Knuth-Morris-Pratt Algorithm

### 1.3.4.  Graph Problems

Informally, a graph is thought of as a collection of points in a plane called "vertices" or "nodes", some of them connected by line segments called "edges" or "arcs".

Formally, a graph **G = {V,E }** is defined by a pair of two sets.

### 1.3.5.  Combinatorial Problems

The traveling salesman Problem and the graph coloring problems are examples of combinatorial problems.

In this problem, a combinatorial object such as a permutation, a combination or a subset that satisfies certain constraints and has some desired property such as maximizes a value or minimizes a cost should be find.

### 1.3.6.  Geometric Problems

Geometric algorithms deal with geometric objects such as point's lines and polygons.

The procedure for solving a variety of geometric problems includes the problems of constructing simple geometric shapes such as triangles, circles and so on.

The two classic problems of computational geometry are the

1.  Closest pair problem
2.  Convex hull problem

The closest pair problem is self explanatory. Given n points in the plane, find the closest pair among them.

The convex hull problem is used to find the smallest convex polygon that would include all the points of a given set.

### 1.3.7.  Numerical Problems

Numerical problems are problems that involve mathematical objects of continuous nature such as solving equations and systems of equations, computing definite integrals evaluating functions and so on. Most of the mathematical problems can be solved approximately.

## 1.4. Time Space Tradeoff

- Efficiency of an algorithm denotes the rate at which an algorithm solves a problem size 'n'.
- It is measured by the amount of resources it uses, the time and the space.

- An algorithm's complexity is measured by calculating the time taken and space required for performing the algorithm.
- The input size denoted by 'n' is one parameter used to characterize the instance of the problem.
- The input size 'n' is the number of registers to hold the input.

### 1.4.1. Time Complexity

Time complexity of an algorithm is the amount of time needed by a program to complete its task.

- The way in which the number of steps required by an algorithm varies with the size of the problem.
- The time taken for an algorithm is comprised of 2 times.
    1. Compilation time
    2. Run time

### 1. Compilation Time

Compilation is the time taken to compile an algorithm.

- While compiling, it checks for the syntax and semantic errors in the particular program.
- It takes own time to compile the program.
- Compilation time is always dependent upon the compiler, since different compilers can take different times to compile the same program.

### 2. Run Time

Run time is the time to execute the compiled program.

- It depends upon the number of instructions present in the algorithm.
- Usually we consider one unit for executing one instruction.
- It is calculated only for executable statements and not for declaration statements.

**Example 1.** Summation of 2 numbers specified by 2 algorithms.

```
Sum1()
{
        Integer x, y, z;
        Read  x, y;
        Z=x+y;
        Print "The sum of x & y", z
```

}

Sum2()

{

    Integer x, y, z;

    Read  x;

    Read  y;

    Z=x+y;

    Print 'The sum of x and y is", z

}

- Consider the 2 algorithm sum 1 ( ) and sum2 () with the statements specified.
- In algorithm sum1 (), we have 4 statements out of which the first statement is a declaration statement and the remaining 3 statements are only executable statements.
- Hence the runtime for the 3 executable statement is 3 units.
- In algorithm sum2(), we have 5 statements out of which the first statement is a declaration statement and the remaining 4 statements are only executable statements.
- Hence the run time for the algorithm sum2 () is 4 units.
- Both the algorithm yields the same results but run time for algorithm are different, since it depends on the number of instructions present in the algorithm.

## *Example 2*

Display 1 to n numbers.

```
void display ()
{
   Int i=1;
   While(i<=n)
    {
     Print i;
     i=i+1;
    }
}
```

- Algorithm display ( ) have 4 statements out of which the first statement is an declaration statement and the remaining 3 statements are executable statements.
- The while loop execute n times and in the $n+1^{th}$ the time the loop terminates.
- While statement executes n+1 time.

- The remaining 2 statements execute n times.
- The total running time is  $\boxed{3n+1}$

## *Time Complexity of an Algorithm is Generally Classified as 3 Types. They are*

1. Worst cast
2. Average case
3. Best case

### *1. Worst Case*

Worst case is the longest time that an algorithm will use over all instances of size n for a given problem to produce a desired results.

- This can be represented by a function $f(n) = n^2$ (or) $f(n) = n \log n$.
- We can write $T(n) = 0(f(n))$
- The algorithm will take no more than f(n) operations.

### *2. Average Case*

- It is the average time that the algorithm will use over all instance of size n for a given problem.
- It depends on the probability distribution of instances of the problem.

### *3. Best Case*

- It is the shortest time that the algorithm will use over all instances of size n for a given problem to produce a desired result.
- We can write $T(n) = \Omega(f(n))$

### *1.4.2. Space Complexity*

Space complexity of a program is the amount of memory consumed by the algorithm until it completes its execution.

The way in which the amount of storage space required by an algorithm varies with the size of the problem to be solved.

### *Types of Memory*

Program uses 2 types of memory such as:

1. Fixed amount of memory
2. Variable amount of memory.

1. **_Fixed Amount of Memory_**

- A fixed amount of memory occupied by the space for the program code and variables used in the program.

2. **_Variable Amount of Memory_**

- A variable amount of memory occupied by the component variable, whose size is dependent on the problem being solved.
- This space increases (or) decreases depending upon whether the program uses interactive or recursive procedures.

**Example 1**: To find the addition of 3 integer numbers

```
Void fun 1()
{
    int  a,b,c,s;
    s=a+b;
    Print "sum : ", S
}
```

The space required by this algorithm

    a=2 units

    b=2 units

    c=2 units

    <u>s=2 units</u>

    8 units

Therefore, this algorithm requires 8 units of memory.

**Example 2**: To find the factorial of a given number.

```
Void fact()
{
    x=1;
    f=1;
    While (x <=n)
    {
    f=x*f;
    x=x+ 1;
}}
```

- The space required by this algorithm

  x =2 units

  f =2 units

  n=2 units
  ___________

  6 units

Therefore, this algorithm requires 6 units of memory.

- Practically time and space complexity can be reduced only to certain levels, the reduction of time increases the space and vice versa. This is known as time space trade off.

**Example 3**: The array contain n elements which are arranged in ascending order. The required output is descending order of n elements.

## *Method 1*

- Use 2 arrays one for input and another for output.
- Read the elements of the first array in reverse linear order.
- Place the elements in second array linearly from the beginning

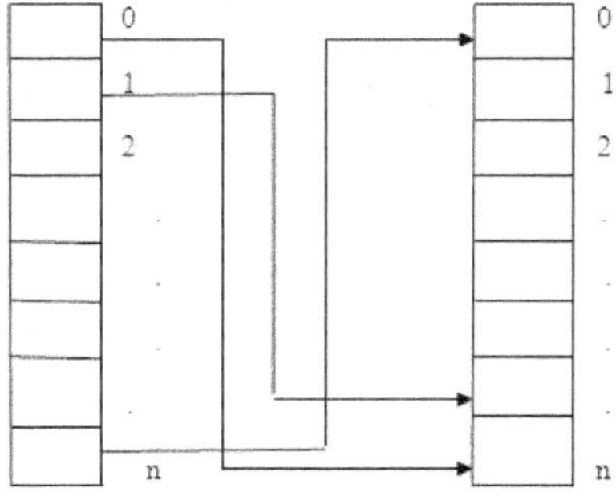

Fig. 1.3: Reversing Array Elements Using 2 Arrays

## *Algorithm*

```
Reverse(n)
{ int ary1 [n];
    int ary2 [n];
    For (int i=0; i<k; i++)
    ary2 [i] = ary1 [(n — 1)—i];
}
```

The space required for this algorithm.

Ary1[n]= n x 2=2n

Ary2[n] = n x 2=2n

i=2

n=2

Therefore, the total space requires for this algorithm 4n +4 = 4(n+1) units of memory.

The total time required for the algorithm = n units of time

### *Method 2*

- It is used to swap the first and last elements.
- Swap the next 2 immediate elements as one from each end and so on.
- This process is repeated until all the elements of the array get swapped.

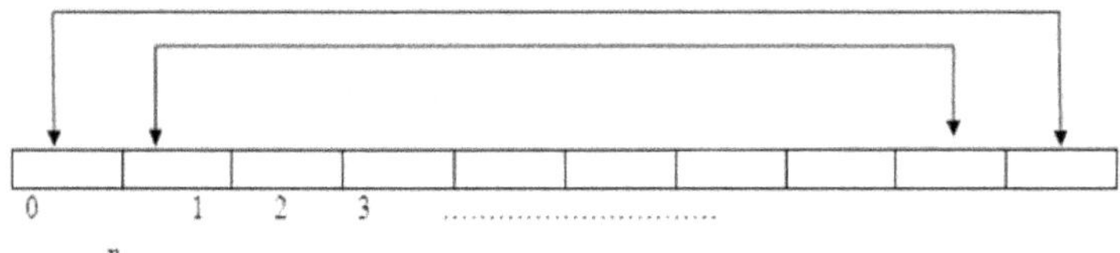

Fig. 1.4: Reversing Array Elements Using Swap Method

### *Algorithm*

```
Reverse(n)
{
    int ary1 [n];
    int k=floor(n/2);
    for (int i=0;i<k;i++)
    swap(& ary  1[i], & ary 1[(n—I) —i]);
}
Swap(int *a, int *b)
{
    int temp =*a;
    *a=*b;
    *b=temp;
}
```

## Space Complexity

Space for ary 1 = n locations.

Space for i, k, temp = 3 locations.

Therefore (All the variable are integer so it require 2n+6 units

## Time Complexity

Each swap requires 3 assignments=3units

No of time swapping =n/2.

∴ Total time = (3n)/2

- In both the methods any attempt in reducing space leads to increase in the time taken by the algorithm and vice versa.
- The first method gave an option of increased space with lesser time.

## 1.5. Asymptotic Notations

Asymptotic notation is a notation which is used to make meaningful statements about the efficiency of a program.

### Types of Notation

3 standard notations are

1. Big oh 0
2. Big omega $\Omega$
3. Theta  $\Theta$

### 1.5.1.  Big oh (0)

### Definition

> A function f(n) is said to be in O(g(n)), if f(n) is bounded above by some constant multiple of g(n) for all large i.e., iff there exists positive constant c and no such that $f(n) \leq c\, g(n)$ for all n> no.

### Example

$100\ n+5\ E\ 0(n^2)$

So 100 n+5 < 100n + n (for all n> 5)

$101n < 101n^2$

C and no, we take 101 and 5

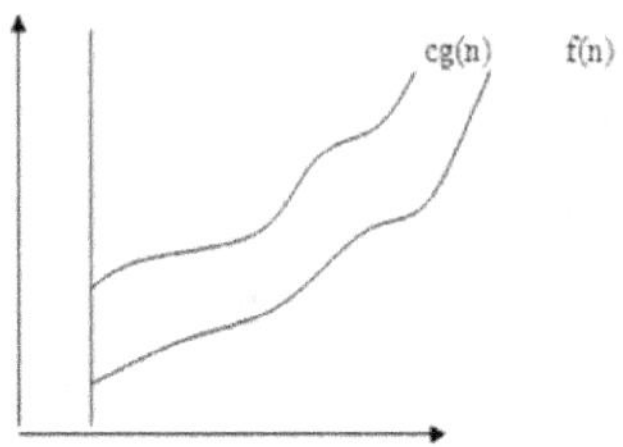

Fig. 1.5: Big oh Notation

### 1.5.2. Big omega (Ω)

A function f(n) is said to be Ω(g(n)) denoted f(n) ε Ω (g(n)) if f(n) is bounded by some constant multiples of g(n) for all large n i.e. if there exists some positive constant c and some non negative integer no such that f(n) ≥c g(n) for  all n≥no.

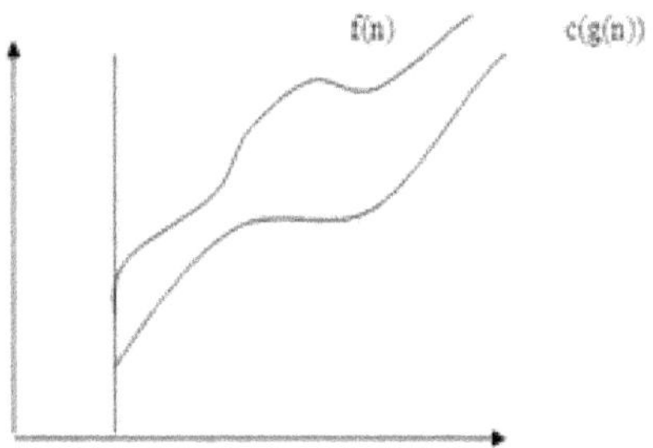

Fig. 1.6: Big Omega Notation f(n) ε Ω(g(n))

### *Example*

$n^3 ε Ω(n^2)$

$n^3 > n^2$ for all n0.

We can select c =1 and n0 =0

### 1.5.3. Theta Notation (θ)

### *Definition*

A function t(n) is said to be in θ(g(n)) denoted f(n) ε θ (g(n)), if f(n) is bounded both above and below by some positive constant multiples of g(n) for all large n. i.e., if there exist some positive constant c1 and c2 and non-negative integer no such that for all n≥n0

$$c_1g(n) \leq f(n) \leq c_2g(n)$$

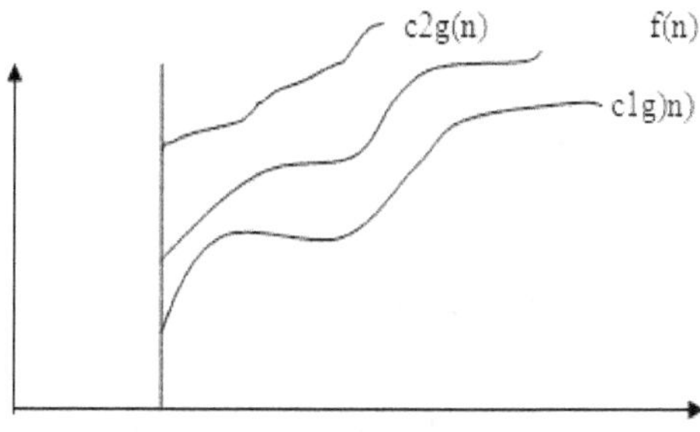


Fig. 1.7: Big theta ε Notation f(n)ε(g(n))

## Example

$$\frac{1}{2}n(n-1) \in o(n^2)$$

$$\frac{1}{2}n(n-1) = \frac{1}{2}n^2 - \frac{1}{2}n \leq \frac{1}{2}n^2 \; for \; all \; n \geq 0$$

(Right in equality (i.e.,) upper bound)

Second we prove the left in equality (the lower bound)

$$\frac{1}{2}n.(n-1) = \frac{1}{2}n^2 - \frac{1}{2}n \geq \frac{1}{2}n^2 - \frac{1}{2}n.\frac{1}{2}n(for \; all \; n \geq 2) = \frac{1}{4}n^2$$

Hence we select $c1 = \frac{1}{4}$ $c2 = \frac{1}{2}$ and $no = 2$

## 1.6. Conditional Asymptotic Notation

### Definition

The asymptotic values of certain functions can be easily derived by imposing certain conditions.

A function f: N —* R≥° is eventually non decreasing if there exists an integer threshold no such that   f (n) ≤ f(n+1) for all n ≥no. This implies by mathematical induction that f(n) ≤f(m) wherever  m≥ n ≥ no.

- Let b > 2 be any integer. Function f is b smooth if, in addition to being  eventually non decreasing, it satisfies the condition f(b(n)) ε 0 (f(n))

- In other words, there must exist a constant c (depending on b) such that f(b(n))≤c f(n) for all n≥ no. A function is smooth if it is b — smooth forever integer b ≥2.

## Property of Smoothness

A useful property of smoothness is that f is b-smooth for any specific integer b≥ 2, and then it is in fact smooth.

- To prove this consider any 2 integers a and b not smaller than 2. Assume that f is b-smooth, We must show that f-is a smooth as well.
- Let c and no be constants such that f(b(n) )≤ c f(n) and f(n) ≤f(n+ 1) for all n≥no.
- Let i = $[log_b a]$ by definition of the logarithm $a = b log_b a - b log_b a = b^i$ consider any n ≥n0.
- It is easy to show by mathematical induction from b — smoothness of f that f($b^i$ n)≤ $c^i$ f(n).But $f(b^i n) \leq f(b^i n)$ because f is eventually non decreasing and $b^i n \geq an \geq n0$
- Most functions in the analysis of algorithms are smooth such as log n, n logn,$n^2$ or any polynomial whose leading coefficient is positive.

## Smoothness Rule

Let f: N⟶ R° be a smooth function and let t : N ⟶ $R^{\geq 0}$ be an eventually non decreasing function. Consider any integer b≥ 2. The smoothness rule asserts that t(n) 0 (f(n)) whenever t(n) ε 0(f(n)) |n is a power of b)

- The rule applies equally to 0 and Ω notation.
- The smoothness rule allow us to infer directly that t(n) ε $\theta(n^2)$ provided, we verify that $n^2$ is a smooth function and t(n) is eventually non decreasing.

## Theorem

Let P ≥ 2 be an integer. Let f, g: N ⟶ $R^{\geq 0}$  Also f be an eventually non decreasing function and g be a p-smooth function. If f(n) ε0 (g(n)) n in a power of P) then f(n) ε O(g(n)).

## Example

Apply the theorem for proving f(n) = O(n log n) $\forall n$, to prove this, we have to prove that f(n) is  eventually non decreasing and n log n in 2-smooth.

Claim (i)-f(n) is eventually non decreasing

- Using mathematical induction, the proof is as follows.

    f(1)=1≤2(1)+2=f(2)

    Assume for all m<n, f(m)≤f(m+1)

    In particular (n/2) ≤f((n+1)/2)

Now,

f(n)=2f(n/2)+n

$\leq 2f((n+1)/2) + (n+1)$

$=f(n+1)$

f (n) is eventually non decreasing

Claim (ii): n log n is 2 — smooth

2n log 2n = 2n (log 2 + log n)

$=O(n \log n)$

Which implies n log n is 2 smooth.

$$\boxed{f(n)= O(n \log n)}$$

## 1.7. Recurrence Equations

### *Definition*

Suppose T (n) is the time complexity of the algorithm for the size of the input n.

Assume that T (n) recursively defined as

$T(n) = b_1 T (n-l) + b_2 T (n-2) +...b_k T (n-K)$

$= a_0 T (n) + a_1 T (n-I) +....a_k T (n-K) =0$

The constant which are bi's are now converted to ai's for simplicity.

Let us denote T (i) as $x^i$, the equation become

$$\boxed{a_0x^k +a_1x^{k-1}+\ldots\ldots\ldots+a^k=0}$$ ecurrence equation

### *Types of Recurrence Equation*

Recurrence equation classified into 2 types.

1.    Homogeneous
2.    Inhomogeneous

- One of the trivial solution for equation $a_0x^n+ a_1 x^{n-1}+........a_k x^{n-k} = 0$

    x=0

    After removing common x terms from this equation, we get

    $a_0x^k + a_1x^{k-1} +.....a^k =0$

which is said to be the characteristic equation, and can have K roots.

- Let the roots be $r_1, r_2 \ldots\ldots r_k$. The roots may or may not be the same.

### Case (i) Suppose All the Roots are Distinct

The general solution is

$$T_{(n)} = \sum c_i \, r_i{}^n$$

Where $c_i$'s are some constant.

### Example

Suppose the characteristic equation is

$x^2 - 5x + 6 = 0$   Find the solution

$x^2 - 5x + 6 = 0$

- $(x-3)(x-2) = 0$
- The roots are 3 and 2

Therefore, The general solution is

$$T(n) = C_i \, 3^n + C_2 \, 2^n$$

### Case (ii) Suppose Some of the p Roots are Equal and the Remaining are Distinct

- Without loss of generality. let us assume that p roots are equal to r1
- The general solution can be stated as

$$T(n) = \sum_{i=1}^{p} c_i \, n^{i-1} \, r_1{}^n + \sum_{i=p+1}^{k} c_i \, r_i{}^n$$

### Example

Suppose the characteristic equation is $(x - 2)^3 \, (x - 3) = 0$. Find the roots.

Then the roots or this equation

$(x-2)\ (x-2)\ (x-2)\ (x-3) = 0$

Roots are 2, 2, 2, & 3

$$T(n) = c_1 \, 2^n + c_2 \, n2^n + c_3 \, n2^2 + c_4 \, 3^n$$

### Inhomogeneous Recurrence Equation

The general form is

$$a_0 \, t_n + a_1 \, t_{n-1} + \ldots\ldots a_1 \, t_{n-k} = b_1{}^n \, P_{1(n)} + b_2{}^n \, P_{2(n)} + \text{where ai's and bi's are constants}$$

Each $P_1(n)$ is a polynomial in n of degree $d_i$

The characteristic equation to be

- $(a_o x^k + a_1 x^{k-1} + \ldots\ldots\ldots\ldots +a_k) \ (x-b_1)^{d1+1} (x-b_2)^{d2+1} \ldots\ldots = 0$
- $(a_o x^k + a_1 x^{k-1} + \ldots\ldots\ldots\ldots +a_k) = 0$
- $(x-b_1)^{d1+t} = 0$
- $(x-b_2)^{d2+1} = 0$

Then the general solution of the in homogeneous equation is given by

$$T(n) = s_1 + s_2 + \ldots\ldots$$

## *Example*

$$f(n) \quad = 2\,f\,(n/2) + n$$

$$f(1) \quad = 1$$

Which is the recurrence equation of the complexity of merge sort aigorithm?

Let $n = 2^k$

For simplicity, we say $f(2^k) = t_k$

$$2\,f^{(n/2)} + n => t_k = 2^t k - 1 \quad = 2^k$$

Which is an inhomogeneous equation?

The characteristic equation of the recurrence equation is

$$(x - 2)\,(x - 2) \ = 0$$

$$=> \quad (x-2)^2 = 0$$

The roots of the equation are 2 and 2 now, the general solution is

$$\boxed{t_k \ = c_1\,2^k \ + c_2\,k_2^k}$$

$$=>f(n)=c_1n+c_2n\log n$$

Given that $f(1) =1=>1=c_1$

$f(2)=2f(1)+2=2+2=4$

$$4=c_1 2+c_2 2$$

$$=>4=2+c_2 2 =>c_2=1$$

$f(n)=n+ n \log n$

$=0 \ (n \log n/ \ n$ is a power of 2)

## 1.8. Solving the Recurrence Equations

### *Solve the Recurrence Equation*

$T(n) - 2T(n-1) = 3^n$ subject to $T(0) = 0$

### *Proof*

The characteristic equation is $(x-2)(x-3) = 0$

Therefore, the roots are 2 and 3

$$T(n) = c_1 2^n + c_2 3^n.$$

Therefore, the general solution is

Since $T(0) = 0$

$T(1) = 3.$

Thus, from the general solution

We get $C_1 = -3$

$C_2 = 3$

So $T(n) = -3 \times 2^n + 3 \times 3^n = \mathbf{0(3^n)}$

Solve the recurrence equation

$T(n) - 2T(n-1) = 1$ subject to $T(0) = 0$

### *Proof*

The characteristic equation is

$(X-2)(X-1) = 0$

Therefore, The roots are 2 and 1

Now the general solution is

$$T(n) = C_1 1^n + C_2 2^n$$

Since $T(0) = 0$

$T(1) = 1$

The general solution we get $C_1= -1$

$C_2=1$

So $T(n)=2^n-1=$ **$O(2^n)$**

## *Solve the Recurrence Equation*

$T(n)=2T(n-1) + n2^n + n^2$

## *Proof*

The characteristic equation is

$(x-2)(x-2)^2(x-3)^3=0$

i.e., $(x-2)^3(x-1)^3=0$

Therefore,   The roots are 2, 2, 2,1,1,1.

Now the general solution is

$T(n) =C_1 2^n+C_2 n2^n+ C_3 n^2 2^n+ C_4 1^n+ C_5 n1^n+ C_6 n^2 1^n$

Hence $T(n)=0(n^2 2^n)$

## 1.9. Analysis of Linear Search

### *Definition-Analysis of Algorithm*

Let Dn be the domain of a problem. Where n be the size of the input. Let $I \varepsilon D_n$ be an instance of the problem, taken from the domain $D_n$. Also take $T(I)$ as the computation time of the algorithm for the instance $I\varepsilon D_n$.

### *1.9.1.   Types of Analysis of Algorithm*

Algorithm can be analyzed into 3 ways.

1.   Best case analysis
2.   Worst case analysis
3.   Average case analysis

### *Best Case Analysis*

- This gives the minimum computed time of the algorithm with respect to all instance, from the respective domain.
- Mathematically, it can be stated as

$$B(n) =\min \{T(I) \varepsilon I\varepsilon Dn\}$$

### *Worst Case Analysis*

- This gives the maximum computation time of the algorithm with respect to all instances from the respective domain.
- Mathematically

$$W(n) = \max\{T(I)\ I\varepsilon D_n\}$$

### *Average case analysis*

- This gives the average computation time of the algorithm with respect to all instances from the respective domain.
- Mathematically, the average case value can be stated as

$$A(n) = \sum P(I)\,T(I)$$

$$I\ \varepsilon\ D_n$$

Where P (I) is the average probability with respect to the instance I.

### *1.9.2. Example for Linear Search*

- We take an array of some elements
- Hence the array is to be searched for the existence of an element x.
- It the element x is in the array, the corresponding location of the array should be returned as an output.
- It the element x is not present in the array, it return -1 as output.

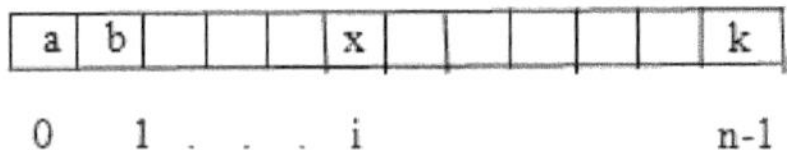

0   1  .   .   . i                     n-1

Fig. 1.8: A Sample Array of Elements

### *1.9.3. Algorithm for Linear Search*

```
int linear search (const char A [ ], const unsigned int size, char ch)
{
for (int i = 0; i < size ; i++)
{
    if(A [i] ==ch)
    return (i);
}
return(-1); }
```

- Here we search the given character in an array.
- Suppose the array contain 5 elements a, e, i, o, u

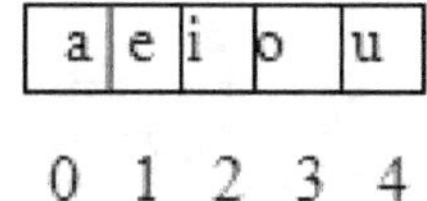

Fig. 1.9: 1 A Sample Array of Character Elements

- If we search the 'i', the algorithm return 2nd location as an output.
- it we search the 'm', the algorithm return -1 as output.

```
int linear search (int A [ ],const unsigned int size, int element)
{
for (int i = 0; i <size; i++)
{
 if(A [i]==element)
 return (i);
}
return (-1);}
```

- Here we search the given element in an array of integer elements.
- The array contain 5 elements 5, 10, 15, 20 & 25

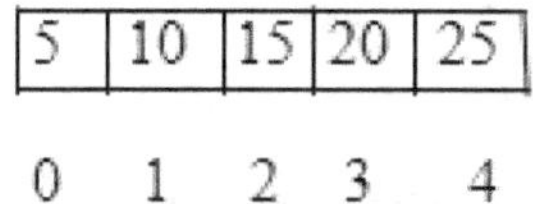

- Suppose, if we search 25, the algorithm return '4' as output.
- If we search 13, the algorithms return - 1 as output.

### 1.9.4. *Comparison of Linear Search*

- The searching process is sequential as one location after the other is searched beginning from the first location to the end of the array.
- The program terminates as soon as it finds the element or fails to find the element in the array after searching the whole array.
- The return value for the successful search is the location of the element x and for an unsuccessful search it is -1.

Table 1.1: Required Number of Comparison for Finding the Element at Version Location

| Location of the element | No of comparisons required |
| --- | --- |
| 0 | 1 |
| 1 | 2 |
| 2 | 3 |
| . | |
| . | |
| . | |
| n-1 | N |
| Not in the array | N |

### *Best Case*

B (n)   = min {1, 2 ... n}

=1

=0(1)

- This is the best case arises when the searching element appears in the first location (0).

### *Worst Case*

W (n) = max { 1, 2, . . . n}

=n

= 0(n)

In the worst case, the element could either be in the last location or could in the array.

### *Average Case*

Let k be the probability of x being in an array.

The average probability is

P ($I_i$) = k/n for $0 \leq i \leq n-1$

P ($I_n$) = 1 - k

The probability for x not being in the array

$$A(n) = \sum_{i=0}^{n} P(Ii)T(Ii)$$

$$=\left( \frac{k}{n} \right) \sum_{i=0}^{n-1}(i + 1)+(1\text{-}k)n$$

$$= \frac{k}{n} \frac{n.(n+1)}{2}+(1\text{-}k)n$$

$$= \frac{k.(n+1)}{2} + (1-k)\,n$$

Suppose x is in the array, then k=1.Therefore,

$$A(n) = \frac{(n+1)}{2} = 0\,(n)$$

In case of x being in the array or not k =1/2

$$A(n) = \frac{(n+1)}{4} + \frac{n}{2}$$

$$= \left(\frac{3}{4}\right) n + 1$$

$$= 0\,(n)$$

Table 1.2: Computation Time for Linear Searching

| Algorithm | Best Case | Worst Case | Average Case |
|---|---|---|---|
| Linear search | O(1) | O(n) | O(n) |

### 1.9.5.  Loop Controls

- The loop control statements in C++ can be classified into 2 categories.

    (1)  Exit control

    (2)  Entry control

### Entry Control

- The while and for loop come under the category of entry control as the condition is verified at the beginning of each iteration.

### For loop

The running time of the for loop

=max {running time of the statements inside the for loop}X no of iterations.

### Example 1

```
int count=0;
For (int i=0;i<n; i++)
        Count++;
```

The running time of the for loop= max {1} X n

$$= n$$

$$= 0\,(n)$$

## Example 2

        int count=0;

        For (int i=0; i<n; i++)

        For (int j=0; j<m; j++)

                Count++;

The running time of the inner loop=m

The running time of the outer loop=O (n,m)

## Example 3

        int count=0;

        For (int i=0; i<n; i++)

                Count++;

        For (int j=0; j<m; j++)

                Count++;

The running time of the $1^{st}$ for loop=n

The running time of the $2^{nd}$ loop=m

Therefore, Total running time is O (n+m)

## Example 4

        int count=0;

        While (count i=n)

                Count + +;

The running time for the while loop = n.

$$= O (n)$$

## Exit Control

- The do while loop come under the category of exit control as the condition is  verified at the end of each iteration.

## Do While Loop

The running time for the do while loop

        = max {running time of the statements inside the do while loop) X no of iterations.

### *Example*

```
int count = 0;

do

{

count ++;

}

while(count<n);
```

Therefore, The running time for this code= 0 (n)

## *If then else Statement*

For the if then else statement

```
If (condition)

Statement 1;

Else

Statement 2;
```

The running time = Time (testing condition) + max {Time (Statement 1), Time (Statement 2))

## *Recursive Call*

```
Unsigned log int Factorial (constant unsigned int n)

{ if(n>=1)

return 1;

else

return n x Factorial (n-1):
```

Time complexity $T(n)= T(n-I) +2$

The value 2 accounts for the testing condition and the computation at the second return statement.

# TWO MARKS QUESTIONS & ANSWERS

## 1. Define Algorithm

An algorithm is a sequence of unambiguous instructions for solving a problem, for obtaining a required output for any legitimate input in a finite amount of time.

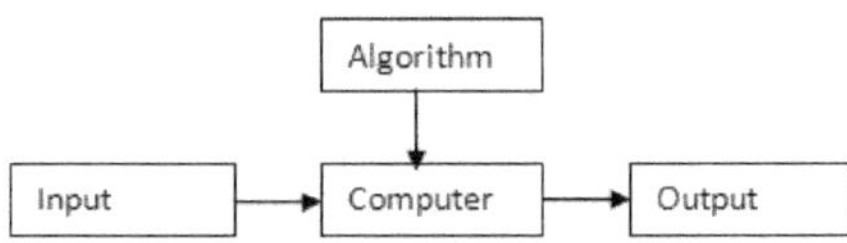


## 2. What are the characteristics of an algorithm?

The important and prime characteristics of an algorithm are

1. **Input:** Zero (or) more quantities externally supplied.
2. **Output:** At least one quantity is produced.
3. **Definiteness:** Each instruction is clear and unambiguous.
4. **Finiteness:** It we trace out the instructions of an algorithm then for all cases , the algorithm terminates after  a finite number of steps.
5. **Efficiency:** Every instruction must be very basic so that it can be carried out in principle by a person using pencil and paper.
6. **Unambiguity:** An algorithm must be expressed in a fashion that is completely free of ambiguity.

## 3. What are 3 parts of the algorithm?

The study of algorithm involves 3 major parts.

- Designing  the algorithm
- Proving the correctness of the algorithm
- Analyzing the algorithm

## 4. What are the criteria used to identify the best algorithm

- Time efficiency
- Space efficiency
- Measuring an input's size
- Units for measuring running time
- Order of growth
- Worst, best and average case efficiencies

5. *What are the sequence steps one goes in designing and analyzing an algorithm?*

- Understanding the problem
- Ascertaining the capabilities of a computational device
- Choosing between the exact and approximate problem solving
- Deciding an appropriate data structures
- Algorithm design techniques
- Methods of specifying an algorithm
- Proving an algorithm correctness
- Analyzing an algorithm
- Coding an algorithm

6. *What are the types of algorithm used to ascertaining the capabilities of a computational device?*

- Sequential algorithm
- Parallel algorithm

7. *What is meant by Sequential algorithm?*

Instructions are executed one after another, one operation at a time. Algorithms of these are designed to be executed on random access machine are called sequential algorithm.

8. *What is meant by Parallel algorithm?*

Random access machine does not hold for some newer computers that can execute operations concurrently in parallel. Algorithm that takes advantage of this capability are called parallel algorithm.

9. *Why would one opt for an approximation algorithm?*

- They are important problems that simply cannot be solved exactly such as extracting square roots, solving non linear equations, and evaluating definite integrals.
- Available algorithms for solving a problem exactly can be unacceptably slow because of the problem's intrinsic complexity.

10. *What is an algorithm design technique?*

An algorithm design technique is a general approach to solving problems algorithmically that is applicable for variety of problems from different areas of computing.

### 11. Define pseudo code?

A pseudo code is a mixture of nature languages and programming languages like constructs. A pseudo code is usually more precise than a natural language and its usage often yields more succinct algorithm descriptions.

### 12. How you analyze an algorithm?

There are two kinds of algorithm efficiency

- Time efficiency – how much extra time memory the algorithm needs.
- Space efficiency – how much extra space the algorithm needs.

### 13. What are the characteristics of an algorithm?

- Simplicity
- Generality

### 14. What are important problem types?

- Sorting
- Searching
- String processing
- Graph problems
- Combinational problems
- Geometric problems
- Numerical problems

### 15. Define sorting?

Sorting is nothing but rearranging the items of a given list in ascending order for this we need to choose a piece of information to guide sorting. This specially chosen piece of information is called a key.

### 16. Define searching?

Searching is finding an element in a given list using a search key.

### 17. Define graph?

Graph is a collection of points called vertices, some of which are connected by line segments called edges.

### 18. What is meant by graph coloring problem?

The graph coloring problem is to assign the smallest number of colors to vertices of a graph so that no two adjacent vertices are of the same color. For example the problem arises in event scheduling. The solution to the graph coloring problem yields an optimal schedule.

### 19. What are combinational problems?

The problems that ask to find a combinational object–such as permutation, a combination or a subset – that satisfies certain constraints and has some desired property.

### 20. What is a geometric algorithm?

Geometric algorithms deal with geometric objects such as points, lines and polygons. This algorithm is used to solve the variety of geometric problems which yields an optimal schedule.

### 21. What are two classic problems of computational geometry? (NOV/DEC 2010)

- Closest-pair problems: The closest-pair problems is self explanatory; given n points in the plane, find the close pair among them.
- The convex hull problem: The convex hull problem asks to find the smallest convex polygon that would include all points of a given set.

### 22. What are numerical problems?

Numerical problems are large special area of applications that involve mathematical objects of continuous nature:

- Solving equations and systems of equations.
- Computing definite integrals
- Evaluating functions

### 23. Define analysis?

American heritage dictionary defines "analysis" as the separation of an intellectual or substantial whole into its constituent parts for individual study.

### 24. How will you find out the efficiency of algorithms?

An Algorithm efficiency can be measured with respect to two resources:

- Running time
- Memory space

# UNIT 2

## Analysis of Sorting and Searching Algorithms

Divide and Conquer – Merge Sort – Quick Sort – Binary Search – Finding Maximum and Minimum – Brute Force – Sequential Search and Brute – Force String Matching – Depth First Search and Breadth First Search.

## Divide and Conquer, Greedy Algorithm

## 2.1. Divide and Conquer

### *Definition*

Divide instance of problem into two or smaller instances and solve smaller instances recursively (though sometimes a different algorithm is employed when instances become small enough) and the solutions obtained for the smaller instances are combined to get a solution to the original instance.

### *Three Steps of the Divide and Conquer Approach*

**Divide** → the problem into two or more smaller sub problems.

**Conquer**→ the sub problems by solving them recursively.

**Combine**→ the solutions to the sub problems into the solutions for the original problem.

### *Rules*

1. An original problem is divided into several sub problems.

2. These sub problems must be solved using recursive algorithm or some other algorithm.

3. Then the solutions of the sub problems are combined to get a solution to the original Problem.

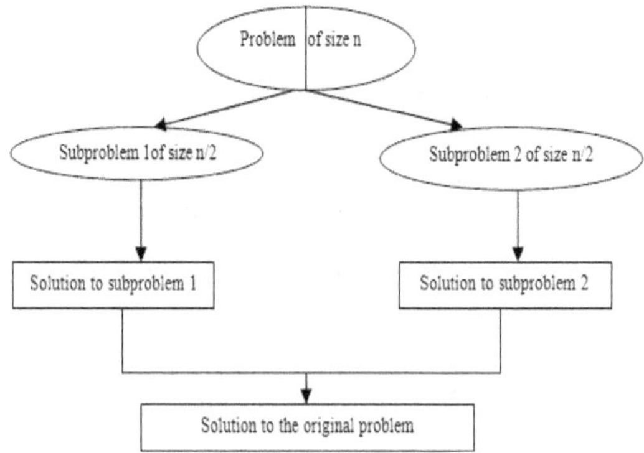


Fig. 2.1: Diagrammatic Representation of Divide and Conquer Technique

### 2.1.1. *General Method*

- Divide the problem p into $P_1$, $P_2$, ..., $P_k$ subproblems until problem p is smaller one.
- Solve the subproblems using recursive algorithm.
- The solution of the problem determine the solution of the  original problem

### 2.1.2. *General Procedure for Divide and Conquer Technique*

Algorithm D and C( P)

{

if Small(P)then return S(P);

// problem is smaller one, it cannot be divided

else

{

    divide P into smaller instances $P_1$, $P_2$, ..., $P_k$, $k \geq 1$;

    apply D and C to each of these subproblems;

    return Combine(D and C($P_1$), D and C($P_2$),..., D and C($P_k$));

}

}

Example:

Computing sum of 'n' numbers

Procedure

- If n>1,we can divide the problem into 2 instances
- To compute the sum of the first [n/2] numbers
- To compute the sum of the remaining [n/2] numbers
- Once the instances are computed, add their values to get the sum of original problem.

$$a_0 + a_1 + \ldots\ldots an\text{-}1 = (a + a + a + \ldots\ldots\ldots a[n/2\text{-}1]) + (a[n/2] + \ldots\ldots an\text{-}1)$$

### 2.1.3. *Complexity of Divide and Conquer Technique*

The complexity of divide and conquer algorithms in given by recurrences of the from

$$T(n)= \begin{cases} T(1) & n=1 \\ aT(n/b) + f(n) & n>1 \end{cases}$$

Where a and b are constants a>1,b>1 n is power of b.

f(n) is a function that accounts for the time spent on dividing the problems into smaller ones and on combining their solution

- T(n) depends on the values of the constant a and b order of the growth of the function f(n)
- One of the method, for solving recurrence relation is called the substitution method.

### *Substitution Method*

- It makes substitution for each occurrence of the function T in the right-hand side until all such occurrences disappear.

**Example:** a = 2,b = 2     let T (1) = 2 &  f(n) = n

$$T(n) = 2T (n/2) + n$$
$$= 2 (2T (n/4) + n/2)+ n$$
$$= 4T (n/4) + 2n$$
$$=8T (n/8) + 3n$$

$$\cdot$$
$$\cdot$$
$$\cdot$$

**$T(n) = 2^i T (n/2^i) + i\,n$**     $\log 2^n \geq i \geq 1$

$T(n) = 2 \log 2^n T (n/2 \log 2^n) + n \log 2^n$

**$T(n) = n \log 2^n + 2n$**

### 2.1.4. *Example for divide and conquer method*

Example for divide and conquer method one

- Binary search.
- Finding maximum and minimum.
- Merge sort.

### 2.1.5. Merits

- The time spent on executing the problem using divide and conquer is smaller than other method.
- It provides efficient algorithm.
- It is ideally suited for parallel computation in which each sub problem can be solved simultaneously by its own processor.

## 2.2. Binary Search

### Concept

Binary search is an efficient algorithm for searching in a sorted array .To search for an element in the list the algorithms split the list and locate the middle element of the list.

### 2.2.1. Procedures for Binary Search Using Divide and Conquer Technique

It works by comparing a search key K with the array's middle element A[m].lf they match, the algorithm stops; otherwise, the same operation is repeated recursively for the first half of the array if K < A[m], and for the second half if K > A[m].

K

$\updownarrow$

A[1].....A[m-1]   A[m]   A[m+1]....A[n]

search if k<A[m]      search if k>A[m]

### 2.2.2. Pseudo Code

if there are no more items to consider then

    Return -1

else

    Set midpoint to (last + first) / 2

if the item at index midpoint = = the target item then

    Return midpoint

else if the item at index midpoint > the target item then

    Return search the left half of the vector (from indices first to midpoint - 1)

else

    Return search the right half of the vector (from indices midpoint + 1 to last).

### 2.2.3.  *Examples for Binary Search*

Binary search for the element x=35 in the array a[1:n]

$$Mid= \left\lceil \frac{low + High}{2} \right\rceil$$

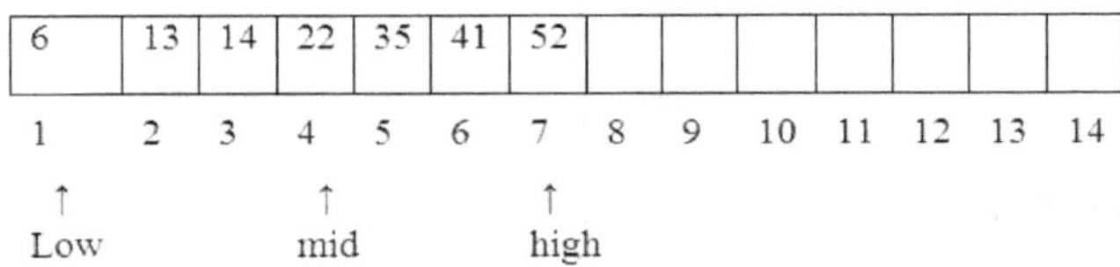

| 6 | 13 | 14 | 22 | 35 | 41 | 52 | 58 | 66 | 72 | 86 | 90 | 92 | 94 |
|---|----|----|----|----|----|----|----|----|----|----|----|----|----|

```
1    2    3    4    5    6    7    8    9    10   11   12   13   14
↑                             ↑                                 ↑
low                           mid                               High
```

Low=1, high=14, mid=(1+14)/2=7

- The search element x is not equal to a[low],a[mid],a[high] but it is less than a[mid] element ie 35<52.
- So the search element is between low to mid ie) 1 to 7 and eliminate from a[8] to a[high].
- low remains same , high =mid , find mid value .

Low=1, high=7,  mid=(1+7)/2=4

| 6 | 13 | 14 | 22 | 35 | 41 | 52 |  |  |  |  |  |  |  |
|---|----|----|----|----|----|----|--|--|--|--|--|--|--|

```
1    2    3    4    5    6    7    8    9    10   11   12   13   14
↑              ↑              ↑
Low            mid            high
```

The search element x is not equal to a[low],a[mid],a[high] but it is greater than a[mid] element ie 35>22.

- So the search element is between mid to high ie) 4 to 7 and omit from a[1] to [3].
- Low=mid ie) low=4, high remains same ie) high=7, find mid value.

Low=4, high=7, mid= (4+7)/2=5

|  |  |  | 22 | 35 | 41 | 52 |  |  |  |  |  |  |  |
|--|--|--|----|----|----|----|--|--|--|--|--|--|--|

```
1    2    3    4    5    6    7    8    9    10   11   12   13   14
              ↑    ↑         ↑
              Low  mid       high
```

The search element x=35 is found at 5th position ie) a [mid] and the search operation completed.

### 2.2.4. *Algorithm*

```
binarySearch(int a[],intn,int x)
//Implements  binary search
//Input: An array a[1: n] sorted in ascending order
// x-search key elements.
//n-number of elements in the list
//if x is present, the function return the position else it returns 0.
{
   low=1;
   high=n;
   while (low<=high)
   {
   mid= (low+high)/2;
   if (x<a[mid])
   high=mid-1;
   else if(x>a[mid])
   low=mid+1;
else
   return (mid);
   }
return (0);
}
```

### 2.2.5. *Complexity of Binary Search*

Complexity of an algorithm is measured in terms of space and time.

### *Space Complexity*

Space required for n elements in an array   = n

Storage for low, mid, high                  =3

Storage for search element x                =1

$$= \boxed{n+4 \text{ locations}}$$

### *Time Complexity*

- The comparison of elements performed by using binary decision tree.
- If search key element x is present, then the algorithm will send at one of the circular node ie) internal node.
- If search key element x is not present the algorithm will end at one of the square node ie) external node.

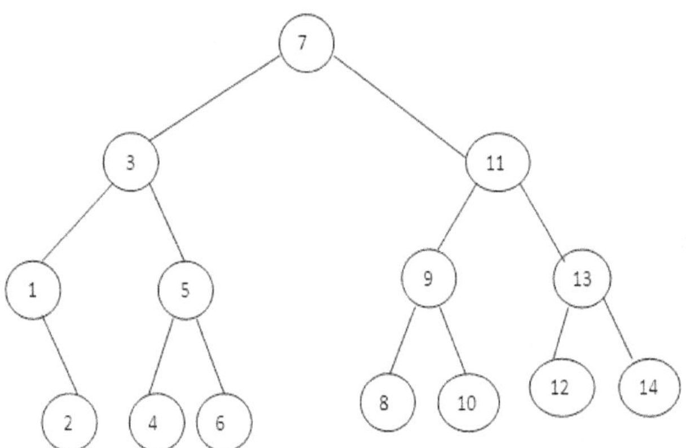

Fig. 2.2: Binary Decision Tree for Binary Search n=14.

### *Best Case*

- The analysis is easy.
- It requires only one comparison.
- The search key element present in the middle element of the array.
- Order of complexity $\boxed{O\,(1)}$

### *Average case*

- It requires only average number of key comparison.
- The order of complexity $\boxed{T\,avg(n)=O(\log_n{}^2)}$

### *Worst case*

- It includes searching of all elements in an array
- It does not contain search key element
- The recurrence relation for Tworst (n) is $\boxed{Tworst\,(n) + O\,\log n}$

### 2.2.6. Merits and Demerits of Binary Search

**Merits**

- In this method elements are eliminated by half each time
- It is faster than the sequential search
- It requires lesser number of key comparison than the sequential search

**Demerits**

- An insertion and deletion of a record requires many records in the existing table be physically moved
- The records are maintain in sequential order
- The ratio between insertion/deletion and search time is very high

## 2.3. Finding Maximum and Minimum

**Concept**

It is used to find the maximum and minimum values of n elements in an array.

The time complexity is computed as the number of element comparisons. The divide and conquer strategy if applied to this problem is more beneficial when it is used on an array of polynomials, vectors, Strings etc.

**This Problem is Discussed with Two Different Approaches**

1. Iterative method
2. Recursive method

### 2.3.1. Procedure for Finding Maximum and Minimum Using Divide and Conquer Technique

- The problem P contain list of n elements $P=(n,a[i],...a[j])$
- If n=1,maximum and minimum=a[1]
- If n=2, it requires only one comparison
- If n>2,it can be divided into 2 instances

    $P_1=((n/2,a[1]....a[n/2])$

    $P_2=((n-(n/2)),a[n/2+1,....a[n])$
- Find max(P) and min(P)
- Max(P) is larger than $max(p_1)$ and $max(p_2)$
- Min(P) is smaller than $min(p_1)$ and $min(p_2)$

### 2.3.2. Algorithm for Maximum and Minimum Using Divide and Conquer Technique

- Maxmin function has 4 inputs lower, upperlimits, max &min element
- If n=-1,maximum and minimum assigned to first location of an array ie max min=a[1]
- If n=2,for finding maximum and minimum  it requires 1 comparison

  if(a[i]<a[j])

  Min=a[i];max=a[j];

  else

  Min=a[j];max=a[j];

- If n>2,find the middle position of an array

  Mid=(i+1)/2

- Call the 2 recursive procedure with following parameters
  1. Maxmin(i,mid,max,min);
  2. Maxmin(mid+1,2,max1,min1);
- Combine the solution

  If (max<max1) max=max1;

  If (min>min1) min=min1;

**Maxmin (i,j,max,min)**

// The arrary contain list of n elements

// i.j are lower and upper limit of an arrary

// max,min are largest and smallest value in a[i,j]

{

// the list contain only one element

if (i==j) then

{

Max=a[i];

Min=a[i];

}

else

```
if (i==j-1) then

//the list contain 2 elements

{

if(a[i]<a[j]) then

{

Max=a[j];

Min=a[i];

}

else

{

Max=a[i];

Min=a[j];

}

}

else

{

//the list contain more than 2 elements

    Mid= (i+l)/2;

//Solve the sub problems

Maxmin( i,midmax,min);

Maxmin(mid+1,j,max1,min1)

//Combine the solutions

if (max<max1) then max=max1;

if(min>min1) then min=min1;

}

}
```

### 2.3.3. Example for Finding Maxmin

**Find the Maximum and Minimum for the Following Set of Elements Using Divide Conquer Technique**

**22 13 -5 -8 15 60 17 31 47**

- $n>2$, So it divide the problem into 2 sets

    $S_1 = \{22, 13, -5, -8, 15\}$

    $S_2 = \{60, 17, 31, 47\}$

- The sets $S_1$ & $S_2$ contain more than 2 elements it divided into 4 subsets

    $S_{11} = \{22, 13, -5\}$

    $S_{12} = \{-8, 15\}$

    $S_{21} = \{60, 17\}$

    $S_{22} = \{31, 47\}$

- The set $S_{11}$ contain more than 2 elements again in divided into 2 sets

    $S_{111} = \{22, 13\}$

    $S_{112} = \{-5\}$

- Find the maximum and minimum for each set
- Compare the maximum and minimum of each set give the maximum and minimum value for entire set
- $S_{112} = \{-5\}$ max & min for this $= \{5\}$
- $S_{111} = \{22,13\}$ max $=22$ & min $=13$
- Combining the solution of $S_{111}$ & $S_{112}$ sets
- $\{-5,13,22\}$

    Max=22

    Min=-5

- $S_{21} = \{60,17\}$

    Maximum & minimum value for this set

    Max= $\{60\}$

    Min= $\{17\}$

- Find the Maximum and minimum value for the set

    $S_{22} = \{31, 47\}$

    Max=47

Min=31

- Find the Maximum and minimum value for the set

    $S_{12}$= {-8, 15}

    Max=15

    Min=-8

- Combining the set $S_{11}$,$S_{12}$

    $S_1$= {22, 13,-5,-8, 15}

    Comparing max of $S_{11}$ with $S_{12,}$ 22 >15

    Max=22

    Comparing min of $S_{11}$ with $S_{12,}$-5 > -8

    So min= -8

- Combining the set $S_{21}$ with $S_{22}$

    Combining max of $S_{21}$ with $S_{22}$   i.e. 60>47, max=**60**

    Combining min of $S_{21}$ with $S_{22}$   i.e. 17<31 min =**17**

- Combining the set $S_1$ and $S_2$

    Comparing max of $S_1$ with $S_2$, i.e. 22<60 so max=**60**

    Comparing min of $S_1$ with $S_2$, i.e. -8<17 so min= **-8**

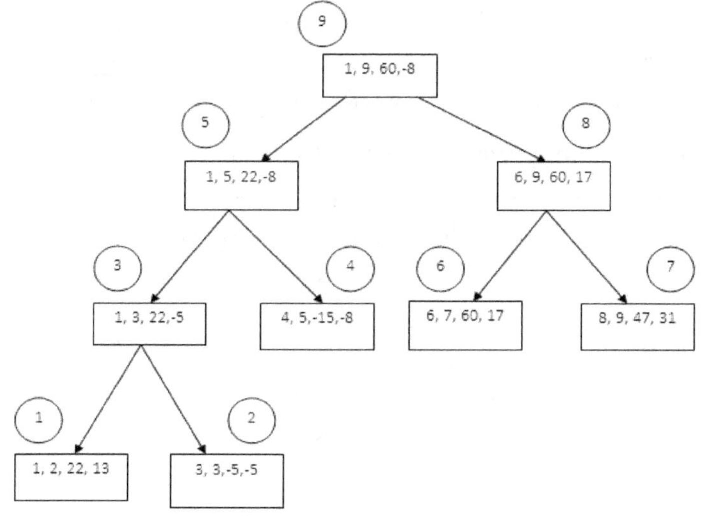

### 2.3.4. *Complexity of Finding Maximum and Minimum*

Complexity of an algorithm is measured in terms of space and time.

### *Space Complexity*

- Given n elements, number of recursion= $(\log_2 n)+1$
- Storage required for each recursion=6+1 values

  ie ( i, j, max, min, max, min, return address.)

### *Time Complexity*

Number of comparison needed for max and min

$$T(n)=\begin{cases} T(n/2)+T(n/2)+2 & n>2 \\ 1 & n=2 \\ 2 & n=1 \end{cases}$$

When n is a power of 2, $n=2^k$ for some positive integer k,

T (n)=2T (n/2) +2

 =2(2T (n/4) +2) +2

 =4T (n/4) +4+2

 =$2^{k-1}+ (2) +\sum_{1\leq k-1} 2^i$

 = $2^{k-1}+ 2^k -2 = \boxed{3n/2\text{-}2}$

Best, average &worst case

The number of comparison needed for all these cases requires $\boxed{3n/2\text{-}2}$

### 2.3.5. *Comparison with Straight Forward Algorithm*

**Straight forward algorithm for finding maximum C minimum**

```
straightmaxmin(a,n,max,min) //set max to maximum,min to minimum
{
max = min = a[1]
for(i=2;i<=n;i++)
{
if( a[i] > max)then
max = a[i];
}
}
```

### *Space Complexity*

| | |
|---|---|
| Space required for n elements in an array | = n |
| Storage space required for max, min, n, i | = 4 |
| Total no of space required for this algorithm | **= n + 4** |

In the case of divide and conquer method it requires storage for 7 elements in each recursion. So it requires more storage space.

### *Time Complexity*

Best, average and worst case–It requires 2n – n comparisons

In the case of divide and conquer approach, it requires 3n/2 – 2 comparison. It reduces 25% of comparison.

### *2.3.6. Merits*

- It is more efficient
- Less number of comparison
- Least cost

## 2.4. Merge Sort

### *Concept*

Merge sort is a perfect example of the divide-and conquer technique. It sorts a given array A[1: n ] by dividing it into two halves (A[1] .. a[n/2]) and (A[n/2+1] .. A[n]). Sort each half individually and then merge the two smaller sorted arrays into a single sorted one.

### *2.4.1. Merge sort Strategy*

- Divide an array into halves.
- Sort each half.
- Merge the sorted halves into one sorted array.

### *2.4.2. Procedure for Merge Sort Using Divide and Conquer Approach*

- To sort an array of n elements, we perform the following steps in sequence
- Divide the list into two sub lists.
- If list have even number of element, split list into two equal sub lists.
- If list have odd number of element, split list into two by making the first sub lists one greater than the second sub lists.

- Then split both sub lists into 2 and go on split until each of the sub lists are of size one.

- Finally start merging the individual sub lists to obtain sorted list.

### 2.4.3. *Mergesort Pseudocode*

mergeSort(int a[], int start, int end)

{

If number of elements to sort is one or fewer, return

Find the middle position

Sort left half (start, middle - 1) //i.e., not  including the middle element

Sort right half (middle, end)

Merge both halves

}

Create a temporary array of the same size as the sum of the two arrays you are combining, for each element of the temporary array, compare elements from each sorted half and assign smallest element to the temporary array.

### 2.4.4. *Algorithm for Merge Sort Using Divide and Conquer Approach*

Mergesort (intlow,int high)

{

if(low<high){

mid=(low+high)/2

mergesort(low,mid);

mergesort(mid+1,high);

//combine the solutions

merge(low,mid,high)

}

Merge(intlow,intmid,int high)

//a[low,high]-sorted array

//two sorted sublists a[low,mid],a[mid+1,high]

//b[]-output

{

h=low;

i=low;

```
j=mid+1;
while((h≤mid)&&(j≤high))
{
if(a[h]<a[j]) then  //compare first position of an array sublists
  {
    b[i]=a[h];
    h=h+1;
  }
else
  {
    b[i]=a[j];
    j=j+1;
  }
i=i+1;
}
if(h>mid)then//copy the remaining elements
{
for(k=j;k<=high;k++)
  {
    b[i]=a[k];
    i=i+1; }}
else
  {
    for(k=h;k<=mid;k++)
      {
        b[i]=a[k];
        i=i+1;
      }
  }
//sorted elements copied into array a
for(k=low;k<=high;k++)
a[k]=b[k];}
```

## *Examples for Merge Sort*

Sort the following elements using merge sort

310,285,175,652,351,423,865,254,450,520

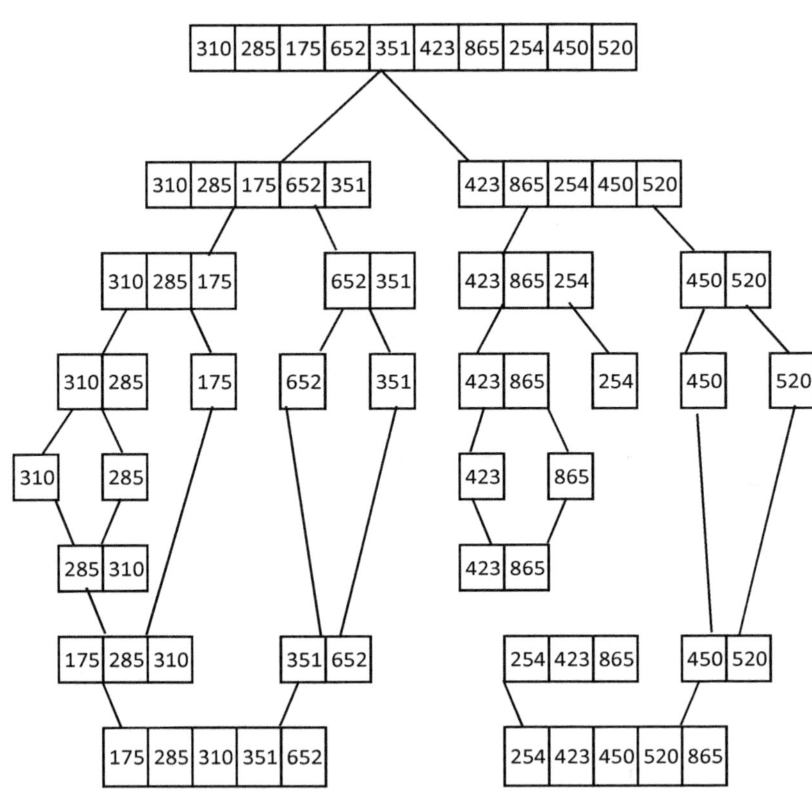

Merging procedure

2 pointers are initialized to point the first elements of the arrays being merged.

| 175 | 285 | 310 | 351 | 652 |   | 254 | 423 | 450 | 520 | 865 |
|-----|-----|-----|-----|-----|---|-----|-----|-----|-----|-----|
| ↑h  |     |     |     |     |   | ↑j  |     |     |     |     |

|   |   |   |   |   |   |   |   |   |   |
|---|---|---|---|---|---|---|---|---|---|
| ↑i |   |   |   |   |   |   |   |   |   |

Compare a[h] and a[j],a[h]<a[j] ie) 175<254,so 175 is copied into array b[],h and i are incremented by one.

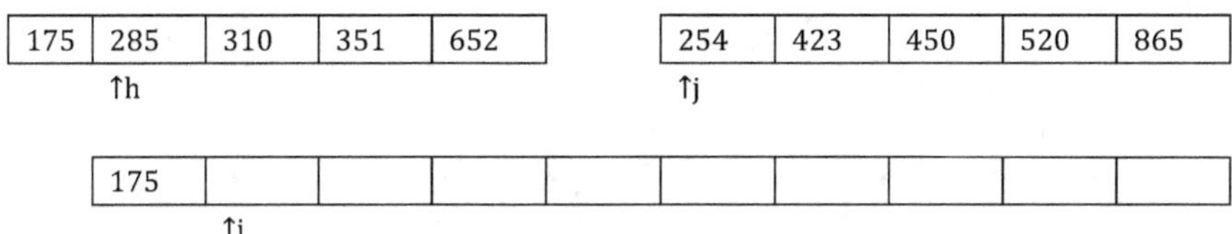

Compare a[h] and a[j],a[h]> a[j] ie) 285>254,so 254 is copied into array b[],j and i are incremented by one.

175 | 285 | 310 | 351 | 652        254 | 423 | 450 | 520 | 865
↑h                                  J

175 | 254
      ↑i

Compare a[h] and a[j],a[h] < a[j] ie) 285 < 423,so 285 is copied into array b[], h and i are incremented by one.

175 | 285 | 310 | 351 | 652        254 | 423 | 450 | 520 | 865
       ↑h                                ↑j

175 | 254 | 285
             ↑i

Compare a[h] and a[j],a[h] < a[j] ie) 310 < 423,so 310 is copied into array b[], h and i are incremented by one.

175 | 285 | 310 | 351 | 652        254 | 423 | 450 | 520 | 865
             ↑h                          ↑j

175 | 254 | 285 | 310
                   ↑i

Compare a[h] and a[j],a[h] < a[j] ie) 351 < 423,so 351 is copied into array b[], h and i are incremented by one.

175 | 285 | 310 | 351 | 652        254 | 423 | 450 | 520 | 865
                   ↑h                    ↑j

175 | 254 | 285 | 310 | 351
                         ↑i

Compare a[h] and a[j],a[h] < a[j] ie) 652 > 423,so 423  is copied into array b[], j and i are incremented by one.

| 175 | 285 | 310 | 351 | 652 |
|-----|-----|-----|-----|-----|

↑h

| 254 | 423 | 450 | 520 | 865 |
|-----|-----|-----|-----|-----|

↑j

| 175 | 254 | 285 | 310 | 351 | 423 |  |  |  |
|-----|-----|-----|-----|-----|-----|--|--|--|

↑i

Compare a[h] and a[j],a[h] < a[j] ie) 652 > 450,so 450  is copied into array b[], j and i are incremented by one.

| 175 | 285 | 310 | 351 | 652 |
|-----|-----|-----|-----|-----|

↑h

| 254 | 423 | 450 | 520 | 865 |
|-----|-----|-----|-----|-----|

↑j

| 175 | 254 | 285 | 310 | 351 | 423 | 450 |  |  |
|-----|-----|-----|-----|-----|-----|-----|--|--|

Compare a[h] and a[j],a[h] < a[j] ie) 652 > 520,so 520  is copied into array b[], j and i are incremented by one.

| 175 | 285 | 310 | 351 | 652 |
|-----|-----|-----|-----|-----|

↑h

| 254 | 423 | 450 | 520 | 865 |
|-----|-----|-----|-----|-----|

↑j

| 175 | 254 | 285 | 310 | 351 | 423 | 450 | 520 |  |
|-----|-----|-----|-----|-----|-----|-----|-----|--|

↑i

Compare a[h] and a[j],a[h] < a[j] ie) 652 <865,so 652  is copied into array b[], h  and i are incremented by one.

| 175 | 285 | 310 | 351 | 652 |
|-----|-----|-----|-----|-----|

↑h

| 254 | 423 | 450 | 520 | 865 |
|-----|-----|-----|-----|-----|

↑j

| 175 | 254 | 285 | 310 | 351 | 423 | 450 | 520 | 652 |  |
|-----|-----|-----|-----|-----|-----|-----|-----|-----|--|

↑i

h > mid ,so the remaining elements of second list copied into array b[].

| 175 | 285 | 310 | 351 | 652 |
|-----|-----|-----|-----|-----|

↑h

| 254 | 423 | 450 | 520 | 865 |
|-----|-----|-----|-----|-----|

↑j

| 175 | 254 | 285 | 310 | 351 | 423 | 450 | 520 | 652 | 865 |
|-----|-----|-----|-----|-----|-----|-----|-----|-----|-----|

The final sorted array contains 175,254, 285, 310,351,423,450,520,652, 865.

### 2.4.5. *Complexity of Merge Sort*

Complexity of an algorithm in terms of time and space.

### *Space Complexity*

Space of merge sort

Each and every recursive call requires stack space for the following elements low, mid, mid+1, high.

### *Space for Merge*

Space for array a and b=2n locations.

Space for control variables h, i, j, k=4

### *Time Complexity*

If the time for the merging operation is proportional to n, then the computing time for merge sort is described by the recurrence relation

$$T(n) = \begin{cases} a & n=1, \text{ a-constant} \\ 2T(n/2)+Cn & n>1, \text{ c-constant} \end{cases}$$

When n is power of 2, $n=2^k$, we can solve this equation by successful substitutions.

T (n)=2(2T (n/4) + (n/2)) +cn

=4T (n/4) +2cn

=2(2T (n/8) +cn/4) +2cn

.

.

.

= $2^k$T (1) +k.cn

= $\boxed{n + c\,n\,\log n}$

if $2^k<n<2^{k+1}$ then $T(n)<=T(2^{k+1})$

therefore T (n) =0 (n log n).

so the merge sort algorithm passes over the entire list and require at most log n passes and merges n element in each pass. The total number of comparison required by the merge sort is

$$\boxed{0 \ (n \log n)}$$

### 2.4.6. Merits and Demerits of Merge Sort

**Merits**

- Guaranteed to run in $\Theta(n \log n)$.
- It requires less running time.
- Used in data processing.

**Demerits**

- Algorithm requires linear amount of extra storage.
- It requires an additional array with n elements
- After merging, the resulting algorithm is quite complicated and also has a significantly larger multiplicative constant.

## 2.5. Brute Force

A straight forward approach, usually based directly on the problem's statement and definitions of the concepts involved.

Brute–force strategy is indeed the one that is easiest to apply.

Examples:

1. Computing $a^n$ (a > 0, n a nonnegative integer)

2. Computing n!

3. Multiplying two matrices

4. Searching for a key of a given value in a list

Brute force method Example

- Selection Sort
- Bubble sort

### 2.5.1. Selection Sort

Scan the array to find its smallest element and swap it with the first element. Then, starting with the second element, scan the elements to the right of it to find the smallest among them and swap it with the second elements. Generally, on pass i $(0 \le i \le n\text{-}2)$, find the smallest element in A[i..n-1] and swap it with A[i]: After $n-1$ passes, the list is sorted.

A[0]  $\le$........ $\le$ A [i-1] | A[i] , ...... . , A[min], ......, A[n-1] in their final positions the last n – i elements pseudo code of this algorithm.

$$
\begin{array}{cccccccc}
|89 & 45 & 68 & 90 & 29 & 34 & 17 \\
17| & 45 & 68 & 90 & 29 & 34 & 89 \\
17 & 29| & 68 & 90 & 45 & 34 & 89 \\
17 & 29 & 34| & 90 & 45 & 68 & 89 \\
17 & 29 & 34 & 45| & 90 & 68 & 89 \\
17 & 29 & 34 & 45 & 68| & 90 & 89 \\
17 & 29 & 34 & 45 & 68 & 89| & 90
\end{array}
$$

## *Algorithm*

```
SelectionSort(A[0..n – 1])
//Sorts a given array by selection sort
//Input: An array A[0..n – 1] of orderable elements
//Output: Array A[0..n – 1] sorted in nondecreasing order
        for i ←0 to n – 2 do
          min←i
        for j ←i + 1 to n – 1 do
          if A[j ]<A[min] min←j
          swap A[i] and A[min]
```

The number of times it is executed depends only on the array size and is given by the following sum:

$$
C(n) = \sum_{i=0}^{n-2} \sum_{j=i+1}^{n-1} 1 = \sum_{i=0}^{n-2} (n - 1 - i) = \frac{(n - 1)n}{2}.
$$

Time efficiency: $\Theta(n^2)$

Space efficiency: $\Theta(1)$, so in place

### 2.5.2. Bubble Sort

Another brute-force application to the sorting problem is

- To compare adjacent elements of the list &exchange them if they are out of order.
- Repeat, till the largest value bubble to the last position on the list.
- The next pass bubbles up the second largest element, and so on.
- After $n – 1$ passes the list is sorted.

## Algorithm

BubbleSort(A[0..n − 1])

//Sorts a given array by bubble sort

//Input: An array A[0....n − 1] of orderable elements

//Output: Array A[0....n − 1] sorted in nondecreasing order

    **for** i ←0 **to** n − 2 **do**

    **for** j ←0 **to** n − 2 − i **do**

    **if** A[j + 1]<A[j ]

    swap A[j ] and A[j + 1]

## Example

## Unsorted Element

| 77 | 42 | 35 | 12 | 101 | 5 |
|----|----|----|----|-----|---|

## First Pass

Compare first & second element ie, 77 & 42.swap the two elements because first element is greater than second

| 77 | 42 | 35 | 12 | 101 | 5 |
|----|----|----|----|-----|---|

**77 > 35 so swap the two values**

| 42 | 77 | 35 | 12 | 101 | 5 |
|----|----|----|----|-----|---|

**77 > 12 so swap the two values**

| 42 | 35 | 77 | 12 | 101 | 5 |
|----|----|----|----|-----|---|

**77 is less than 101 No need to swap**

| 42 | 35 | 12 | 77 | 101 | 5 |
|----|----|----|----|-----|---|

**101 > 5 so swap the two values**

| 42 | 35 | 12 | 77 | 101 | 5 |
|----|----|----|----|-----|---|

| 42 | 35 | 12 | 77 | 5 | 101 |
|----|----|----|----|---|-----|

*Second Pass*

| 42 | 35 | 12 | 77 | 5 | 101 |
|----|----|----|----|---|-----|

| 35 | 42 | 12 | 77 | 5 | 101 |
|----|----|----|----|---|-----|

| 35 | 12 | 42 | 77 | 5 | 101 |
|----|----|----|----|---|-----|

| 35 | 12 | 42 | 77 | 5 | 101 |
|----|----|----|----|---|-----|

| 35 | 12 | 42 | 5 | 77 | 101 |
|----|----|----|---|----|-----|

| 35 | 12 | 42 | 5 | 77 | 101 |
|----|----|----|---|----|-----|

$$T(n) = c_1(n+1) + c_2 \sum_{i=1}^{n}(n-i+1) + c_3 \sum_{i=1}^{n}(n-i) + c_4 \sum_{i=1}^{n}(n-i)$$

$$= \Theta(n) + (c_2 + c_2 + c_4) \sum_{i=1}^{n}(n-i)$$

$$\text{where } \sum_{i=1}^{n}(n-i) = \sum_{i=1}^{n}n - \sum_{i=1}^{n}i = n^2 - \frac{n(n+1)}{2} = \frac{n^2}{2} - \frac{n}{2}$$

$$\text{Thus, } T(n) = \Theta(n^2)$$

Time efficiency: $\Theta(n^2)$

### 2.5.3. Sequential Search Algorithm

This algorithm simply compares successive elements of a given list with a given search key until either a match is encountered (successful search).The list is exhausted without finding a match (unsuccessful search).

*Algorithm*

SequentialSearch2(A[0....n], K)

//Implements sequential search with a search key as a sentinel

//Input: An array $A$ of $n$ elements and a search key $K$

//Output: The index of the first element in $A[0..n-1]$ whose value is

// equal to $K$ or $-1$ if no such element is found

     A[n]←K

     i ←0

     **while** A[i] _= K **do**

      i ←i + 1

     **if** i < n **return** i

     **else return** −1

The searching in such a list can be stopped as soon as an element greater than or equal to the search key is encountered.

*Time efficiency: O(n)*

### 2.5.4. String Matching

Pattern: a string of m characters to search for

Text: a (longer) string of n characters to search in problem: find a substring in the text that matches the pattern

### Brute-force Algorithm

**Step 1:** Align pattern at beginning of text

**Step 2:** Moving from left to right, compare each character of pattern to the corresponding character in text until

- all characters are found to match (successful search); or
- a mismatch is detected

**Step 3:** While pattern is not found and the text is not yet exhausted, realign pattern one position to the right and repeat Step 2

*Examples of Brute-Force String Matching*

Pattern: 001011

Text: 10010101101001100101111010

Pattern: happy

Text: It is never too late to have a happy childhood.

## Algorithm

```
BruteForceStringMatch(T [0.....n – 1] , P[0....m – 1])
//Implements brute-force string matching
//Input: An array T [0....n – 1] of n characters representing a text and
// an array P[0..m – 1] of m characters representing a pattern
//Output: The index of the first character in the text that starts a
// matching substring or –1 if the search is unsuccessful
        for i ←0 to n – m do
        j ←0
           while j <m and P[j]= T [ i + j ] do
                j ←j + 1
           if j = m return i
        return –1
```

## 2.6. Graph Traversal

### Concept

A more general form is to determine for a given starting vertex $v \in V$ all vertices such that there is a path from v to u. It starts at initial vertex and visits each and every vertex exactly once and finally reaches an end vertex.

Searching a vertex in a graph can be solved by starting at vertex v and systematically searching the graph G for vertices that can be reached from, u.

### Types of Traversal

Graph traversal can be classified into 2 types.

1.  Breadth first search and traversal.
2.  Depth first search and traversal.

### 2.6.1. Breath First Search and Traversal

#### Concept

- It starts from arbitrary vertices.
- It visits all vertices adjacent to starting vertex
- Then it visits all unvisited vertices.
- This process is repeated until no vertex is left.

#### Procedure for Breath First Search

- It starts at initial vertex and mark it as having been visited.
- The vertex V is at this time said to be unexplored.
- The vertex V is said to explored, if its adjacent vertices are visited.
- All unvisited vertices adjacent from V are visited next. these vertices are unexplored vertices.
- The newly visited vertices have not been explored and are put on to the end of a list of unexplored vertices.
- Exploration continues until no unexplored vertex is left.

#### Queue

- Queue is used to trace the breath first search (BFS)
- Queue is initialized with the traversal's starting vertex, which is marked as visited.
- The unvisited vertices that are adjacent to the front vertex are marked as visited and it is added to the queue.
- The front vertex is removed from the queue.

#### Example for Breadth First Search and Traversal

#### Example 1

Find the BFS for the following undirected graph.

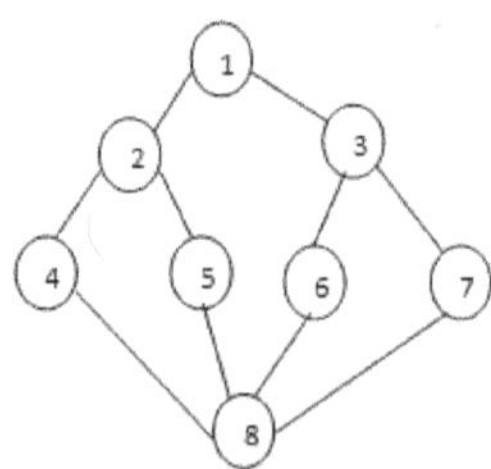

Fig. 2.3: Undirected Graph

- Algorithm starts from initial vertex ie node 1, it is visited, but it is unexplored and put into the queue.

| 1 | |
|---|---|

- The adjacent vertices for 1 are 2 and 3. Next these nodes are visited, but they are unexplored, put into the queue.
- Now the node 1 is explored and it is removed from the queue.

| ~~1~~ | 2 | 3 | |
|---|---|---|---|

- It process the next vertex 2. The adjacent vertices for 2 are 1,4,5. 1 is already, visited, then 4 and 5 are visited, but they are unexplored, put into the queue.

| 2 | 3 | 4 | 5 | |
|---|---|---|---|---|

- Now the node 2 is explored and it is removed from the queue.

| ~~2~~ | 3 | 4 | 5 | |
|---|---|---|---|---|

- It process the next vertex ie 3. The adjacent vertices for 3 are 1 6 7 1 already visited, so the vertex 6 and 7 are visited but they are unexplored vertices, put into the queue.

| ~~3~~ | 4 | 5 | 6 | 7 | |
|---|---|---|---|---|---|

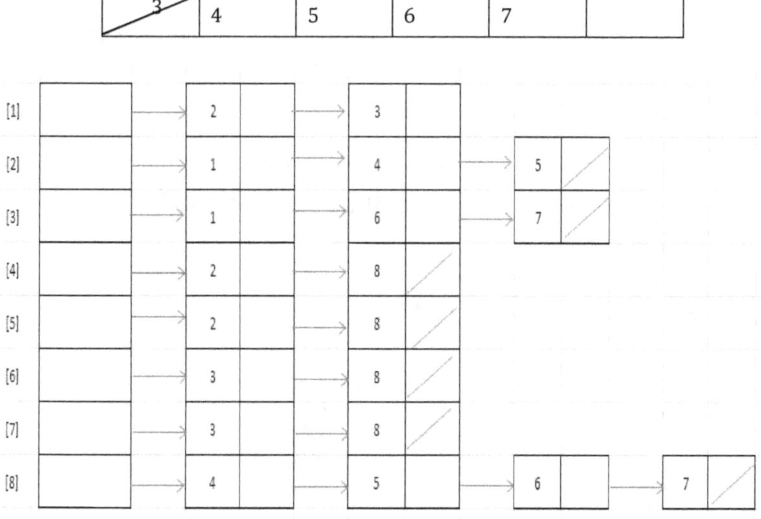

- Now the node 3 is explored and it is removed from the queue.

| ~~3~~ | 4 | 5 | 6 | 7 |
|---|---|---|---|---|

- It process is next vertex 4. The adjacent vertices for 4 are 2 and 8 2 is already visited, so it visits the vertex 8 8 is unexplored vertex and it is put into the queue.

- Now, the node 4 is explored and it is removed from the queue.

- It process the next vertex ie 5. The adjacent vertices for 5 are2 and 8, both 2 and already visited. So node 5 is explored and it is removed from the queue.

| 5 | 6 | 7 | 8 | |
|---|---|---|---|---|

- It process the next vertex ie 6. The adjacent vertices for 6 are 3 and 8, both 3 and 8 are already visited, so node 6 is explored and it is removed from the queue.

| 4 | 5 | 6 | 7 | 8 | |
|---|---|---|---|---|---|

- It process the next vertex ie 7. The adjacent vertices for 7 are 3 and 8, both 3 and 8 are already visited, so node 7 is explored and it is removed from the queue.

| 6 | 7 | 8 | |
|---|---|---|---|

| 7 | 8 | |
|---|---|---|

- It process is next vertex ie 8. The adjacent vertices for 8 are 4, 5, 6 and 7.All the vertices are already visited. So node 8 is explored and it is removing from the queue.

| 8 | |
|---|---|

- Therefore, The vertices visited in the order of 1,2,3,4,5,6,7 &8.

## Example 2

### Find the BFS for the following Directed Graph

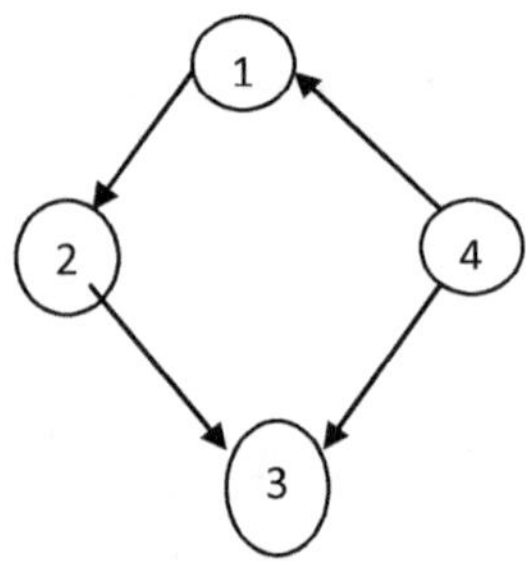


- Find the adjacency list for the above graph

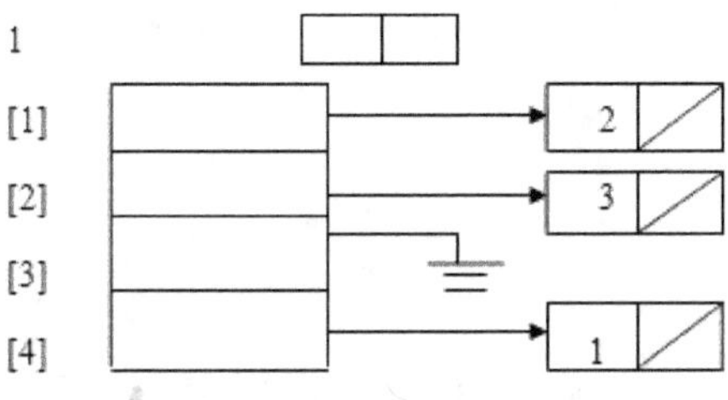

- Algorithm starts form the initial vertex ie node 1, it is visited but it is unexplored and put into the queue.
- The adjacent vertices for 1 are 2. Node 2 is visited, but it is unexplored put into the queue.

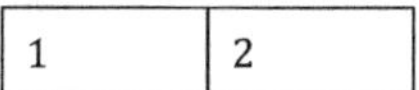

- Vertex 1 is explored and it is removed from the queue
- It process the next vertex ie 2. The adjacent vertices for node 2 is3.Node 3 is visited but it is unexplored and put into the queue.

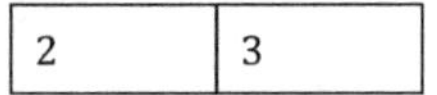

- Vertex 2 is explored and it is removed from the queue.

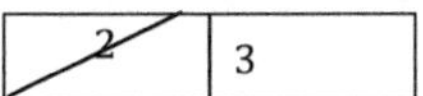

- It process the next vertex is 3. These are no adjacent vertices for node 3. Node 3 is explored and it is removed from the queue.

- Vertex 4 is not reached from 1.All the vertices visited in the order 1,2, & 3.

### Algorithm for Breadth First Traversal

Void BFT (G,n)

//G is a graph

//n is number of vertices

{

for(i=1; i<=n; i++)

//mark all vertices unvisited.

Visited [i]=0;

```
for(i=1;i<=n; i++)

if( visited [i] = 0)

BFS (i);

}

Void BFS (v)

//A BFS of G is carried out beginning at vertex V.

For the node i, visited [i] = 1

//the node i has been already visited.

// q contains unexplored vertices.

{

u=V;

visited [v] =1

repeat

{

for all vertices w adjacent from u do

{

if (visited [w]== 0)

{

add w to 1; // q is unexplored

visited [W] = 1;}}

if(q is empty)

return // no unexplored vertex.

Delete the next element, u from q

//Get first unexplored vertex

}

until (false);}
```

*Complexity for Breadth First Search*

*Space Complexity*

| | |
|---|---|
| Space is needed for array visited | = n locations |
| Space for queue | = n-1 |
| Remaining variable | = 1 |
| Space for the Total space | = n + n locations |

*Time Complexity*

If the graph G is represented by adjacency matrix representation it requires $O(n^2)$ time.

If the graph G is represented by adjacency list representation it requires **O (IVI + l EI)** time.

## 2.6.2. Depth First Search and Traversal

*Concept*

- It starts at arbitrary vertex V.
- The exploration of a vertex V is suspended as soon as a new vertex is reached.
- At this time the exploration of the new vertex u begins.
- When this new vertex has been explored the exploration of V continues.
- The search terminates when all reached vertices have been fully explored.

*Procedure*

1. It starts visiting vertices of a graph arbitrarily by making it has visited.
2. On each iteration, the algorithm proceeds with unvisited adjacent vertex.
3. The algorithm stops, when there is no unvisited adjacent vertex.
4. Then the algorithm backs up one edge to the vertex it came from and tries to continue visiting unvisited form there.
5. The algorithm halts, when there are no unvisited vertexes.

*Stack Representation*

- Stack is used to trace the operation of DFS.
- Push a vertex on to the stack, when the vertex is reached for the first time.
- Pop a vertex from a stack, when it becomes dead end.

### *Examples for Depth First, Search and Traversal*

### *Example 1*

Find DFS for the following undirected graph.

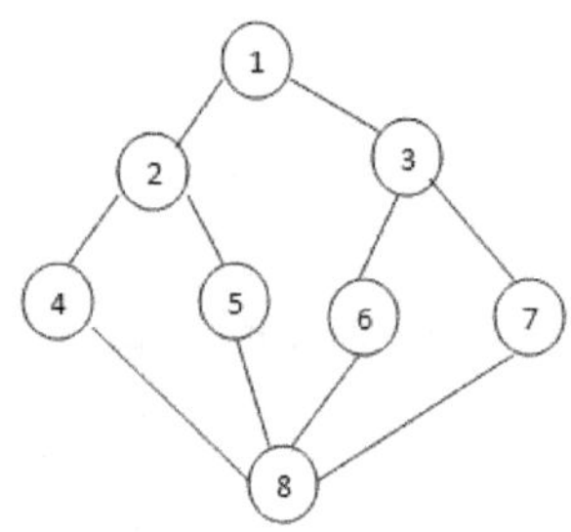

It starts with vertex 1

From 1 →2→4→ 8→5

From 5 traversal stops, since there are no unvisited vertexes, so it goes back to 8.

From 8→6→3→7

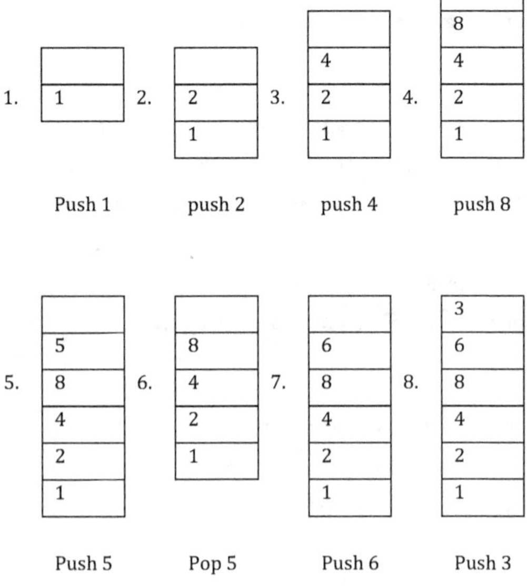

|  | 9. | | 10. | | 11. | | 12. |
|---|---|---|---|---|---|---|---|
| | 7 | | 3 | | 6 | | 8 |
| | 3 | | 6 | | 8 | | 4 |
| | 6 | | 8 | | 4 | | 2 |
| | 8 | | 4 | | 2 | | 1 |
| | 4 | | 2 | | 1 | | |
| | 2 | | 1 | | | | |
| | 1 | | | | | | |

|  | Push 7 | Pop 7 | Pop 3 | Pop 6 |

|  | 13. | | 14. | | 15. | | 16. |
|---|---|---|---|---|---|---|---|
| | 4 | | | | | | |
| | 2 | | 2 | | | | |
| | 1 | | 1 | | 1 | | |

|  | Pop 8 | Pop 4 | Pop 2 | Pop 1 |

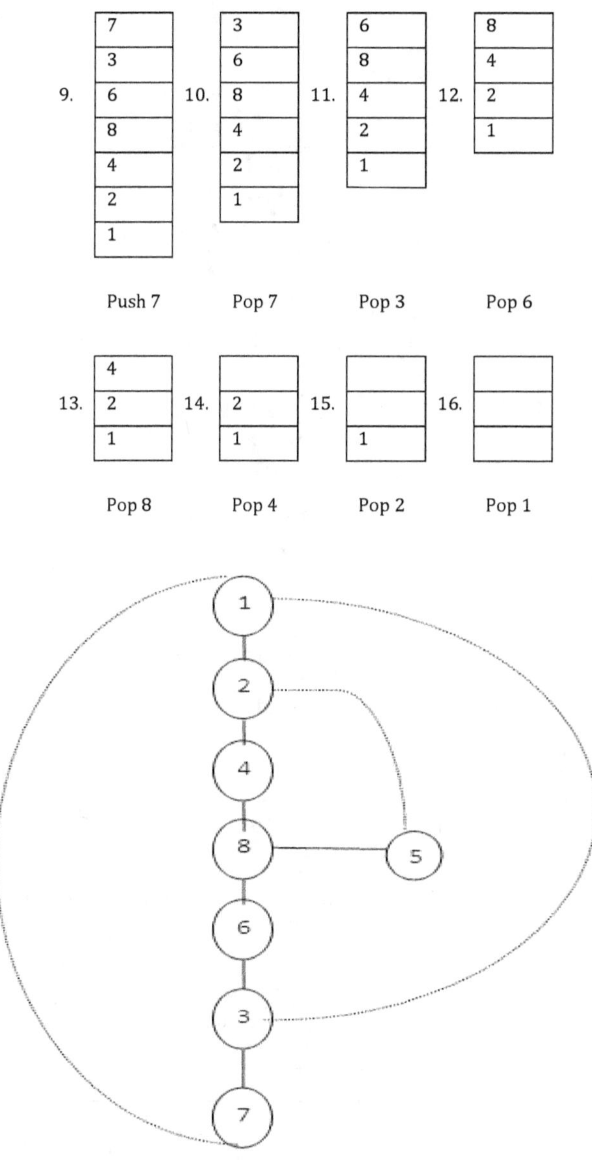

Fig. 2.4: Depth First Search First

## Example 2

### Find DFS for the Following Graph

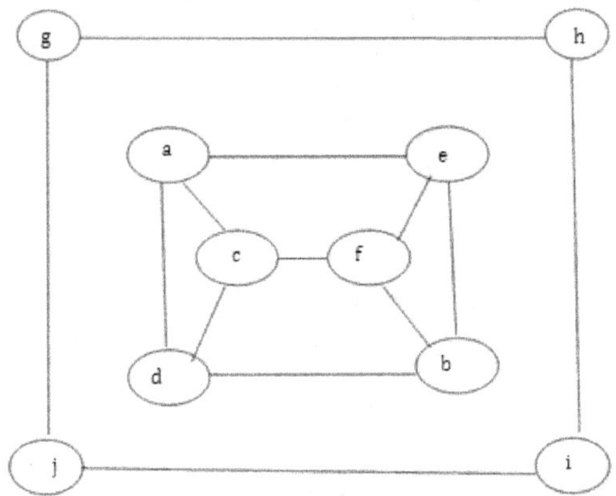

- It starts with vertex a

From a→c→f→b→e

From e, traversal stops ,since there no unvisited vertex ,so it goes back to c.e

From c→d, traversal stops, since there no visited vertex

It goes to g→h→i→j

Stack shows the above example

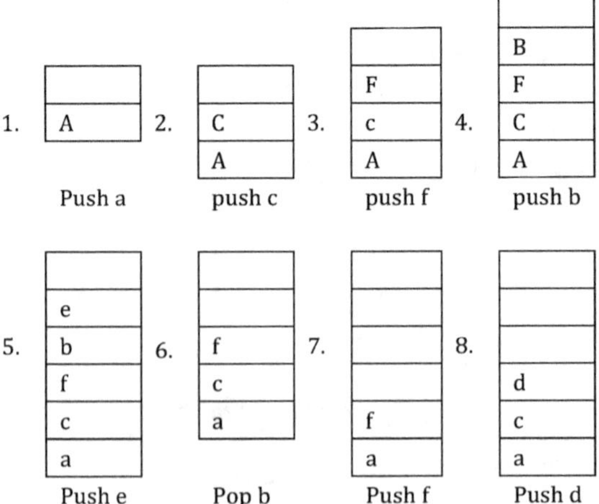

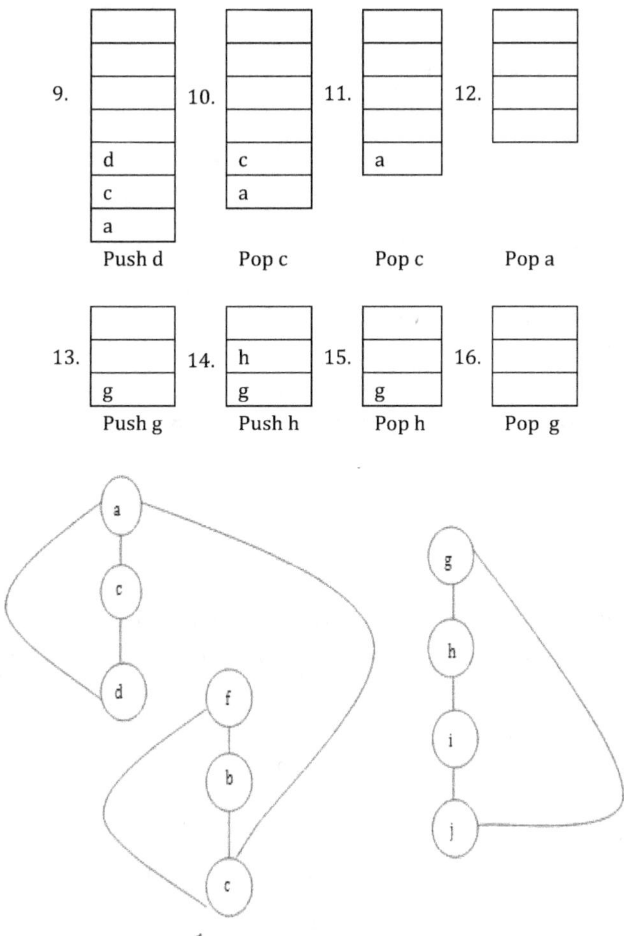



Fig. 2.5: Depth First Search

## *Algorithm for Depth First Search*

void DFS (V)

// Given an undirected graph G =(V,E)

//Graph G contain n vertices

//Array visited [] initially set to zero.

// The algorithm visits all  vertices reachable from v

{

Visited[v]=1;

for  each vertex w adjacent from V do

{

If(visited[w]==0)

DFS(w);

}

}

### Complexity for Depth First Search

### Space Complexity

| | |
|---|---|
| Space is  needed for array visited | = n locations |
| Space for calling DFS (ie space for DFS recursion) | = 2*n=2n |
| Total space | =3n |

### Time Complexity

- If the graph G is represented by adjacency matrix represented it requires $O(n^2)$ time.
- If the graph G is represented by adjacency list representation, it requires $O(|V|+|E|)$ time

### Similarities between DFS and BFS

| Factors | DFS | BFS |
|---|---|---|
| Data structure | Stack | Queue |
| Number of vertex | 2 ordering | 1 ordering |
| Edge types | Tree edge | Tree edge |
| | Back edge | Cross edge |
| Applications | 1.Connectivity | 1.Connectivity |
| | 2. acyclicity | 2.acyclicity |
| | 3 .Articulation points | 3.Minimum edge paths |
| Efficiency of adjacent matrix | $\Theta(|v^2|)$ | $\Theta(|v^2|)$ |
| Efficiency for adjacent Linked list | $\Theta(|v|+|E|)$ | $\Theta(|v|+|E|)$ |

# Two Mark Questions and Answers

## 1. What are the objectives of sorting an algorithm?

The objectives of sorting an algorithm are

(1) To rearrange the items based on its key

(2) To search an element in the list

## 2. What is meant by optimal solution(may/june'07)

Given a problem with n inputs , We obtain a subset that satisfies some constraints .Any subset that satisfies these constriants is called a feasible solution.

A feasible solution which either maximizes or minimizes a given objectives function is called optimal solution.

## 3. Find the best case and worst case for binary search

### Best Case

- The analysis is easy.
- It requires only one comparison.
- The search key element present in the middle element of the array.
- Order of complexity $O(1)$.

### Average Case

- It requires only average number of key comparison.
- The order of complexity $T\,avg(n) = O\,(\log_n^2)$

### Worst Case

- It includes searching of all elements in an array
- It does not contain search key element
- The recurrence relation for Tworst (n) is $Tworst\,(n) + O\,\log n$

## 4. Define knapsack problem

We are given n objects and a knapsack or bag. Object i has a weight $w_i$ and the knapsack has a capacity m. if a fraction $x_i, 0 \le x_i \le 1$.of object 'i' is placed into the knapsack, then a profit $p_i x_i$ is earned.

The objective is to obtain a filling of the knapsack that maximizes the total profit earned.

## 5.  Define divide and conquer algorithm

Divide instance of problem into two or smaller instances and solve smaller instances recursively (though sometimes a different algorithm is employed when instances become small enough) and the solutions obtained for the smaller instances are combined to get a solution to the original instance.

### Three steps of the divide and conquer approach

**Divide** → the problem into two or more smaller subproblems.

**Conquer**→ the subproblems by solving them recursively.

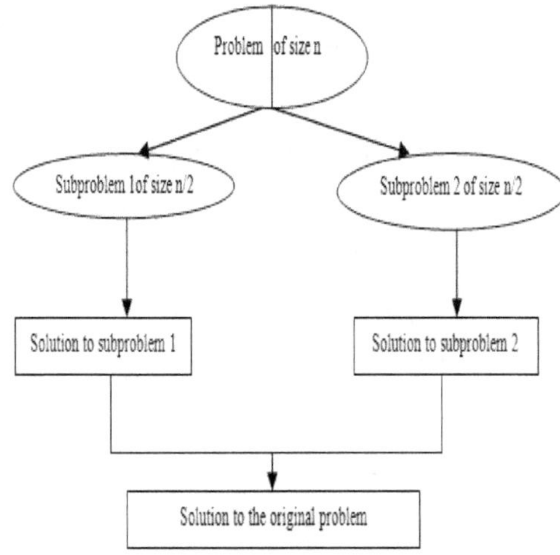


## 6.  Give some examples for divide and conquer method

Example for divide and conquer method one

1.  Binary search.
2.  Finding maximum and minimum.
3.  Merge sort.

## 7.  What are the merits and demerits of binary search?

### Merits

- In this method elements are eliminated by half each time
- It is faster than the sequential search
- It requires lesser number of key comparison than the sequential search

*Demerits*

- An insertion and deletion of a record requires many records in the existing table be physically moved
- The records are maintain in sequential order
- The ratio between insertion/deletion and search time is very high

## 8. Define merge sort

Merge sort is a perfect example of the divide-and conquer technique. It sorts a given array A[1: n ] by dividing it into two halves (A[1] .. a[n/2]) and (A[n/2+1] .. A[n]).

Sort each half individually and then merge the two smaller sorted arrays into a single sorted one.

## 9. What are the merits and demerits of merge sort?

*Merits*

- Guaranteed to run in $\Theta(n \log n)$.
- It requires less running time.
- Used in data processing.

*Demerits*

- Algorithm requires linear amount of extra storage.
- It requires an additional array with n elements
- After merging, the resulting algorithm is quite complicated and also has a significantly larger multiplicative constant.

## 10. Define greedy concept.

Greedy technique constructs a solution to an optimization problem by piece by piece through a sequence of choice that are:

- Feasible
- Locally optimal
- Irrevocable

For some problems, yields an optimal solution for every instance. For most, does not but can be useful for fast approximations.

### 11. Define container loading

A large ship is to be loaded with cargo. The cargo is containerized and all containers are the same size. Different containers may have different weights. $w_i$ be the weight of the $i^{th}$ container $1 \leq i \leq n$.

The cargo capacity is C. Based on the greedy concept load the ship with the maximum number of containers.

### 12. What is the complexity of container loading?

Complexity of an algorithm in terms of time and space.

### Space Complexity

Space for weight of n containers stored in an array c[ ] = n locations

Space for indication of container loading stored in an array x[ ] = n locations

Capacity of cargo c = 1 location

Numbers of containers 'n' = 1 location

Control variable 'i' = 1 location

Therefore, total space required = **2n + 3**

### Time Complexity

(1) Sorting the container increasing order of their weight = O(log n)
   Using merge sort

(2) Algorithm for loading of container = O(n)
   Therefore, time complexity = **O(n log n)**

### 13. Define complexity of knapsack problem

### Space Complexity

Space for profit array  = n locations

Space for weight array = n locations

Space for solution array = n locations

Capacity of knapsack m = 1 location

Numbers of objects 'n' = 1 location

Control variable 'i' = 1 location

Therefore, total space required =  **3(n + 1)**

## *Time Complexity*

Sorting the order = O( n)

Algorithm for filling the knapsak = O(n)

Therefore, time complexity = **O(n )**

# Unit 3

## Greedy Algorithms

Greedy Algorithms: General Method – Container Loading – Knapsack Problem - Prim's Algorithm – Kruskal's Algorithm – Dijkstra's Algorithm – Huffman trees.

## 3.1. Greedy Technique

Greedy technique is an approach, which is applied for change making problem.

The Greedy technique suggests constructing a solution to an optimization problem through a sequence of steps, each expanding a partially constructed solution obtained so far, until a complete solution to the problem is reached.

On each step, the choice made must be feasible, locally optimal and irrevocable.

Feasible: It has to satisfy the problem's constraints

Locally Optimal: It has to be the best local choice among all feasible choices available on that step.

Irrevocable-Once made, it cannot be changed on subsequent steps of the algorithm.

## 3.2. Container Loading

### Concept

A large ship is to be loaded with cargo. The cargo is containerized and all containers are the same size. Different containers may have different weights. $w_i$ be the weight of the $i^{th}$ container $1 \leq i \leq n$.

The cargo capacity is C. Based on the greedy concept load the ship with the maximum number of containers.

### Procedure for Container

The ship may be loaded in stages.

- At each stage we need to select a container to load
- Select the container with least weight
- Check each time before the loading of container C[i] .weight <= capacity
- The process is repeated until it reaches cargo capacity 'C'.

### Feasible Solution

Every set of $x_i$'s (container) that satisfies the constraints $\sum^n w_i x_i < C$ then $x_i$ assigned to value 1. Otherwise it is assigned to $\Phi$     $i=1$

$\sum^n w_i x_i < = C, x_i \in \{0,1\}, 1 \le i \le n$

$i=1$

where $w_i$ – weight of the container 'i'.

$x_i$ – value of the container is assigned to '0' (or) 1.

If the container is loaded, it is assigned to 1, otherwise it is $\Phi$. C – cargo capacity

n – no of containers in cargo

### Optimal Solution

- Load the ship with the maximum number of containers
- Every feasible solution that maximum the $\sum^n x_i$ function is an optimal solution i=1

### Examples for Container Loading

The cargo contain 8 container n=8. weight of the containers $\{w_1, w_2, w_3 \ldots \ldots w_8\} = \{100,200,50, 90,150,50,20,80\}$ and containers of the cargo is 400. Find optimal solution for loading the containers,

1. Arrange the containers in ascending order of their weights $\{7,3,6,8,4,1,5,2\} = \{20,50,50, 80,90,100,150,200\}$. Initially none of the containers will not be loaded. The solution set becomes $\{0,0,0,0,0,0,0,0\}$

2. In stage 1, the container 7 is selected, whose weight is 20. Check the constraint $\sum w_i <=$ c.ie $20 <= 400$ the container 7 is loaded, $x_7$ value is assigned to 1. Therefore value of the solution set $=\{0,0,0,0,0,0,1,0\}$

3. In stage 2, the container 3 is selected, whose weight is 50. Check the constraint $\sum w_i <=$ c.ie $50 + 20 < 400$ $70 <= 400$ the, $x_3$ value is assigned to 1. Therefore value of the solution set $=\{0,0,1,0,0,0,1,0\}$

4. In stage 3, the container 6 is selected, whose weight is 50. Check the constraint $\sum w_i <=$ c.ie $120 <= 400$ the container 4 is loaded, $x_4$ value is assigned to 1. Therefore value of the solution set $=\{0,0,1,0,0,1,1,0\}$

5. In stage 4, the container 8 is selected, whose weight is 80. Check the constraint $\sum w_i <=$ c.ie $200 <= 400$ the container 8 is loaded, $x_8$ value is assigned to 1. Therefore value of the solution set $=\{0,0,1,0,0,1,1,1\}$

6. In stage 5, the container 4 is selected, whose weight is 90. Check the constraint $\sum w_i <= c$.ie $290 <= 400$ the container 4 is loaded, $x_4$ value is assigned to 1. Therefore value of the solution set $=\{0,0,1,1,0,1,1,1\}$

7. In stage 6, the container 1 is selected, whose weight is 100. Check the constraint $\sum w_i <= c$.ie $390 <= 400$ the container 1 is loaded, $x_1$ value is assigned to 1. Therefore value of the solution set $=\{1,0,1,1,0,1,1,1\}$

8. In stage 7, the container 5 is selected, whose weight is 150 .Check the constraint $\sum w_i <= c$.ie $540 <= 400$ the container 5 is not loaded. Therefore optimal solution $\sum x_i = 6$.

### *Algorithm for Container Loading*

```
void container loading (container *c, int capacity, int no of containers, int *x)

// c is the capacity of containers

{

//sort the containers in ascending order of their weights

Sort (c, noofcontainers);

n= noofcontainers;

//initialize the variables x

for(i=1;i<=n;i++)

x[i]=0;

i=1;

//select the containers in order of their weight

While (i<=n && c[i]<= capacity)

{

//c[i] weight of the container i

x[i] = 1;//the container I is loaded.

Capacity = capacity – c[i]; //remaining capacity of the cargo

i++;

}

}
```

*Complexity of Container Loading*

Complexity of an algorithm in terms of time and space.

*Space Complexity*

Space for weight of n containers stored in an array c[ ] = n locations

Space for indication of container loading stored in an array x[ ] = n locations

Capacity of cargo $\quad\quad\quad$ c = 1 location

Numbers of containers $\quad$ 'n' = 1 location

Control variable $\quad\quad\quad$ 'i'= 1 location

Therefore, total space required = $\quad$ 2n + 3

*Time Complexity*

Sorting the container increasing order of their weight using merge sort = O(log n)

Algorithm for loading of container = O(n)

Therefore, time complexity = O(n log n).

## 3.3. Knapsack Problem

*Concept*

We are given n objects and a knapsack or bag. Object i has a weight $w_i$ and the knapsack has a capacity m. if a fraction $x_i$, $(0 \le x_i \le 1)$ of object 'i' is placed into the knapsack, then a profit $p_i x_i$ is earned.

The objective is to obtain a filling of the knapsack that maximizes the total profit earned.

*Feasible Solution*

Any set$(x_1, x_2, \dots x_n)$, satisfy the constraint

$$\sum_{1 \le i \le n} w_i x_i <= M$$

x is assigned to 0, fraction 0 or 1 $\quad 0 \le x_i \le 1,\ 1 \le i_i \le n$

Where wi-weight of the object i

xi-fraction of object i

m-capacity of the knapsack.

## Optimal Solution

It is feasible solution which maximizes the function

$$\sum_{1 \leq i \leq n} p_i x_i$$

Where $p_i$ is the profit of the object i.

## Procedure for Knapsack Problem

- Arranging n objects in ascending order of profit/weight ratio.
- Select the object and check the constraint $\sum w_i <= m$
- Based on the capacity of the knapsack, complete or fraction n of object added to the knapsack.
- Find $\sum p_i x_i$ after adding object into the knapsack.
- This process is repeated, until it reaches capacity of the knapsack.

## Example for the Knapsack Problem

Consider the following instance of the knapsack problem n=3, m=20

(p1,p2,p3)=(25,24,15),(w1,w2,w3)=(18,15,10).

## Find Optimal Solution

## Solution

- Arrange the objects in ascending order of profit / weight ratio.

  (1.6,1.5,1.3) = (15,10,18) = (02,03,01)

- In stage 1, object 2 is selected.

- Check the constraints $\sum w_i <= m$. ie 15<20 so object 2 completely added into the knapsack

- Find $\sum p_i x_i$ (ie) 24 x 1 = 24.

- In stage 2, object 3 is selected.

- Check the constraints $\sum w_i <= m$.ie 10 > 5.so only half of the object 3 added into the knapsack

- Find $\sum p_i x_i$ (ie) 24 x 1 + ½ x 15= 31.5.

Optimal solution is 31.5.

### Algorithm for Knapsack Problem

```
Greedy knapsack (m,n)
//p[1:n] and w[1:n] contain the profits and weights
//object are arranged in their profit/weights ratio
   m- capacity of the knapsack
//x [1:n] solution Vector
{
for(i=1;i<=n;i++)
x[i]=0.0
//initially none of the object is added.
U=m;
for(i=1;i<=n;i++)
{
if(w [i] > U) then
break;
x[i]=1.0;
U=U-w[i];
}
if( i<=n) then
x[i] = U/w[i];
}
```

### Complexity of Knapsack Problem

Complexity of an algorithm in terms of time and space.

### Space Complexity

Space for profit array = n locations

Space for weight array = n locations

Space for solution array = n locations

Capacity of knapsack m = 1 location

Numbers of objects 'n' = 1 location

Control variable 'i' = 1 location

Therefore, total space required = **3(n + 1)**

### *Time Complexity*

Sorting the order=O( n)

Algorithm for filling the knapsak=O(n)

Therefore, time complexity=**O(n )**

## 3.4. Prim's Algorithm

Prim's Algorithm works for obtaining minimum spanning tree. Let us first understand the concepts of spanning tree and minimum spanning tree.

### *Spanning Tree*

A spanning tree of a graph G is a sub graph which is basically a bee and it contains all the vertices of G containing no circuit.

### *Minimum Spanning Tree*

A minimum spanning tree of a weighted connected graph G is a spanning tree with minimum or smallest weight.

### *Weight of the Tree*

A weight of the tree is defined as the sum of weights of all its edges.

For example:

Consider a graph G as given below. This graph is called weighted connected graph because some weights are given along every edge and the graph is a connected graph.

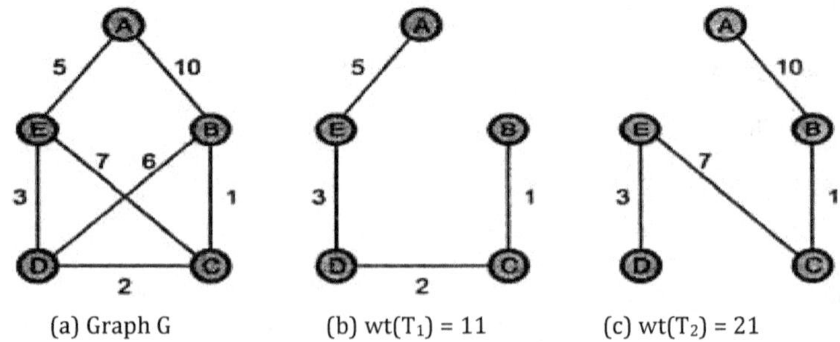

<table>
<tr><td>(a) Graph G</td><td>(b) wt(T$_1$) = 11</td><td>(c) wt(T$_2$) = 21</td></tr>
</table>

Fig. 3.1: Graph and Two Spanning Trees Out of which (b) is a Minimum Spanning Tree

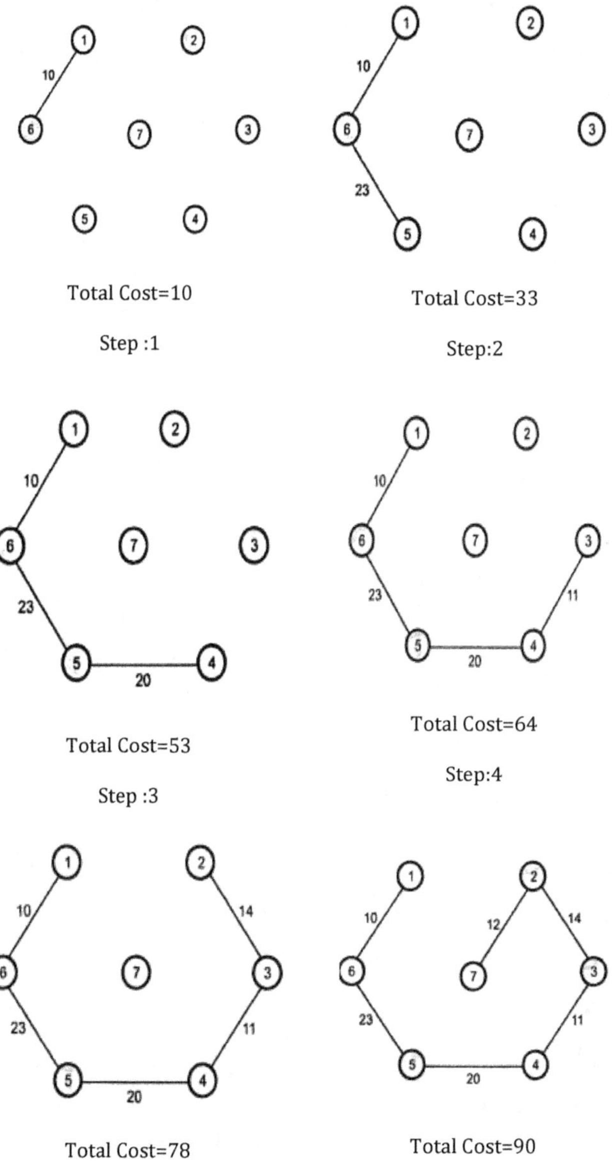


Total Cost=10
Step :1

Total Cost=33
Step:2

Total Cost=53
Step :3

Total Cost=64
Step:4

Total Cost=78
Step:5

Total Cost=90
Step:6

***Routine for Prim's Algorithm***

```
void Prims(Table T)

{

Vertex v,w;

for(i=0;i<numvertex;i++)

{

T[i].Known=false;

T[i].Dist=Infinity;

T[i].Path=0;

}

for(;;)

{

Let V be the start vertex with the smallest distance

T[v].dist=0;

T[v].known=True;

For each w adjacent to V

if(!T[w].Known)

{

T[w].Dist=min(T[w].Dist,Cvw);

T[w].Path=V;

}}}
```

## 3.5. Kruskal's Algorithm

Kruskal's algorithm is another algorithm of obtaining minimum spanning tree. This algorithm is discovered by a second year graduate student Joseph Kruskal. In this algorithm always the minimum cost edge has to be selected. But it is not necessary that selected optimum edge is adjacent

Difference between Prim's and Kruskal's Algorithm

| Prim's Algorithm | Kruskal's Algorithm |
| --- | --- |
| This algorithm is for obtaining Minimum spanning tree by selecting the vertices of already selected vertices. | This algorithm is for obtaining minimum spanning tree but it is not necessary to choose adjacent vertices of already selected vertices. |

Let us understand this algorithm with the help of some example.

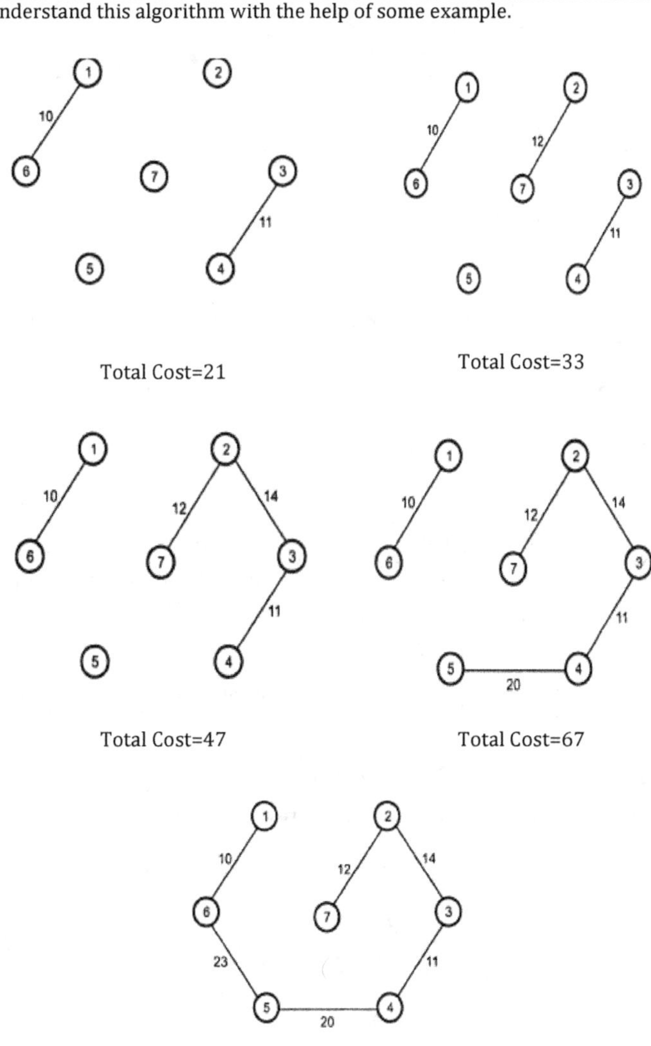

Total Cost=21

Total Cost=33

Total Cost=47

Total Cost=67

Total Cost=90

*ALGORITHM Kruskal(G)*

// Kruskal's algorithm for construction a MST

// Input: A weighted connected graph G=[V,E]

//Output: $E_T$, the set of edges composing a MST(G) sort E in nondecreasing order of the edge weight w(ei1)<=.....<=w(ei$_{|E|}$)

$E_T$ =NULL;

count=0;

K=0;

While count<|V|-1 do

K=k+1;

If $E_T$U{$e_{ik}$} is acyclic

   $E_T$ =$E_T$ U{eik};

count=count+1;

   Return $E_T$;

## 3.6. Dijkstra's Algorithm

Dijkstra's Algorithm is a popular algorithm for finding shortest path. This algorithm is called single source shortest path algorithm. In this algorithm, for a given vertex called source the shortest path to all other vertices is obtained. In this algorithm the main focus is not to find only one single path but to find the shortest paths from any vertex to all other remaining vertices. This algorithm applicable to graphs with non-negative weights only.

Dijkstra's algorithm finds shortest paths to graph are vertices in order of their distance from a given source. In this process of finding shortest path, first it finds the shortest path from the source to a vertex nearest to it, then second nearest and so on.

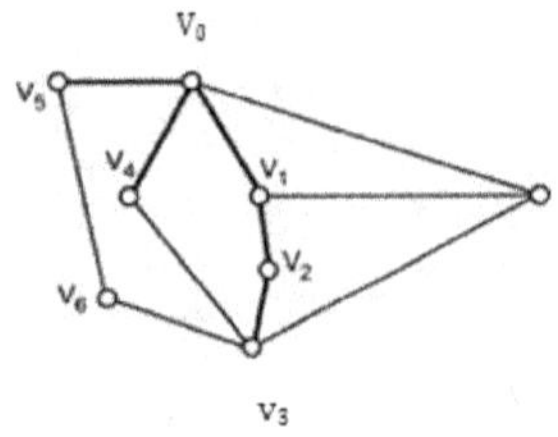

The shortest path from $V_0$ is obtained. First we find shortest path from $V_0$-$V_1$ then $V_1$-$V_2$ then from $V_2$-$V_3$ the shortest distance is obtained. Let us understand this algorithm with some example.

Consider a weighted connected graph as given below.

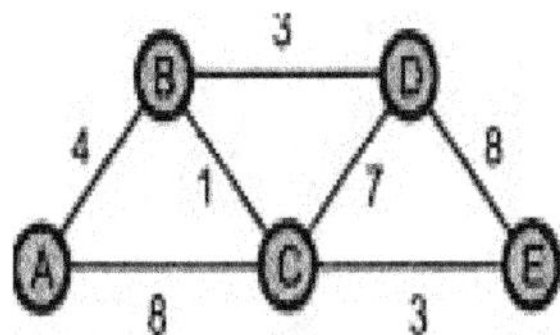

Now we will consider each vertex as a source and will find the shortest distance from this vertex to every other remaining vertex. Let us start with vertex A.

| Source Vertex | Distance with other vertices | Path shown in graph |
|---|---|---|
| A | A-B,    path = 4<br>A-C,    path = 8<br>A-D,    path = ∞<br>A-E    path = ∞ | |
| B | B-C,    path = 4 + 1<br>B-D,    path = 4 + 3<br>B-E    path = ∞ | |
| C | C-D,    path = 5 + 7 = 12<br>C-E,    path = 5 + 3 = 8 | |
| D | D-E,    path = 7 + 8 = 15 | |

But we have one shortest distance obtained from A to E and that is A-B-C-E with path length = 4+1+3=8.

Similarly other shortest paths can be obtained by choosing appropriate source and destination.

### *Routine for Dijkstra's Algorithm*

```
void Dijkstra(Table T)

{

Vertex v,w;

for(i=0;i<numvertex;i++)

{

T[i].Known=false;

T[i].Dist=Infinity;

T[i].Path=0;

}

for(;;)

{

Let V be the start vertex with the smallest distance

T[v].dist=0;

T[v].known=True;

For each w adjacent to V

if(!T[w].Known)

{

T[w].Dist=min (T[w].Dist,T[V].dist+Cvw);

T[w].Path=V;

}

}

}
```

## 3.7. Huffman Trees

A Huffman tree is a binary tree that minimizes the weighted path length from the root to the leaves containing a set of predefined weights.

The most important application of Huffman trees are Huffman Codes.

A Huffman code is a optimal prefix tree variable length encoding scheme that assigns bit strings to characters based on their frequencies in a given text. This is accomplished by a greedy construction of a binary tree whose leaves represent the alphabet characters and whose edges are labeled with 0's and 1's.

To encode a text that comprises n characters from some alphabet by assigning to each of the text's characters some sequence of bit called the code word.

### *Fixed Length Encoding*

Is assigns to each character a bit of string of the some length m(m>=logn)

### *Variable Length Encoding*

It assigns code words of different lengths to different characters.

### *Prefix Free Code or Prefix Code*

In a prefix code no codeword is a prefix of a codeword of other characters.

To construct a tree that would assigns shorter bit strings to high frequency characters and longer ones to low frequency characters and longer ones to low frequency characters can be done by greedy algorithm invented by David Huffman.

### *Huffman's Algorithm*

### *Step 1*

Initialize n one node trees and label them with the characters of the alphabet. Record the frequency of each character's in its tree's root to indicate the tree's weight.

### *Step 2*

Repeat the following operation until a single tree is obtained. Find two trees with the smaller weight. Make them, the left and right subtree of a new tree and record the sum of their weights in the root of the new tree as its weight.

A tree constructed using Huffman algorithm is called Huffman tree.

## *Example*

Consider the five alphabet {A,B,C,D,-} with the following occurrence probabilities.

| Character | A | B | C | D | - |
|---|---|---|---|---|---|
| Probability | 0.35 | 0.1 | 0.2 | 0.2 | 0.15 |

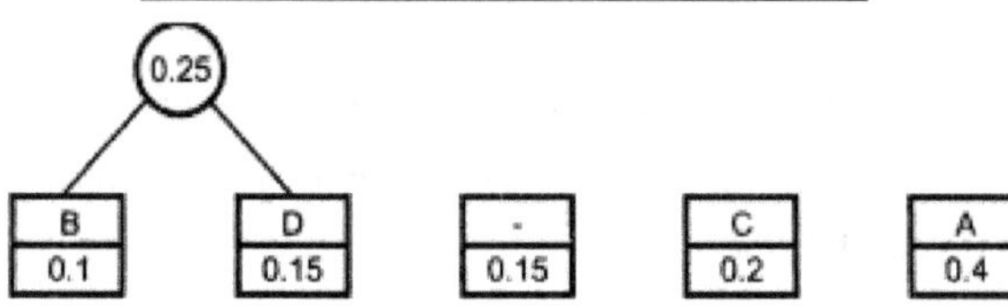

Rearrange the nodes in ascending order.

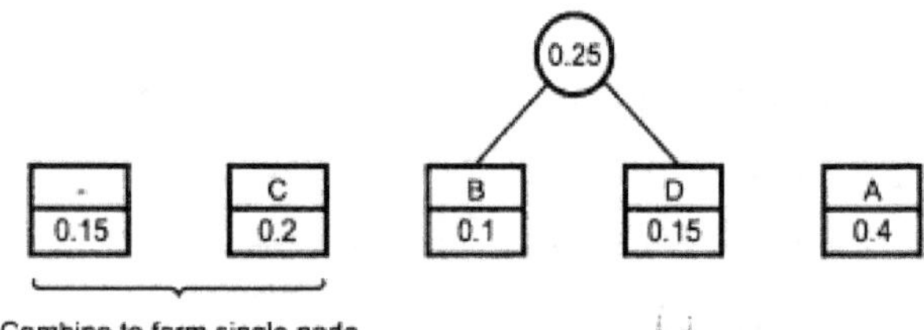



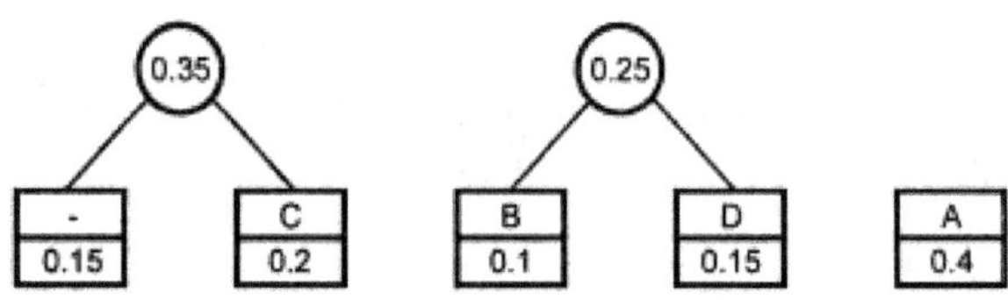



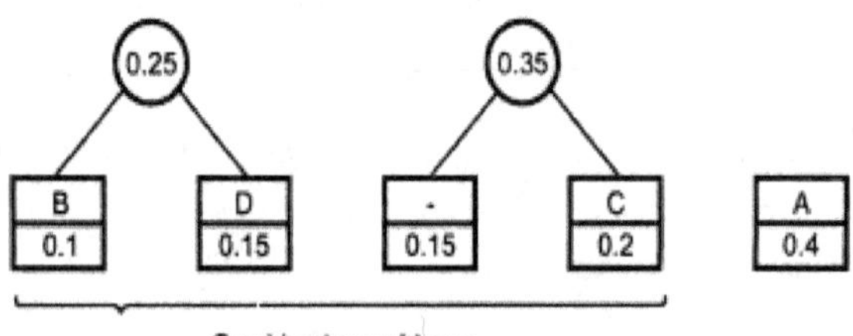

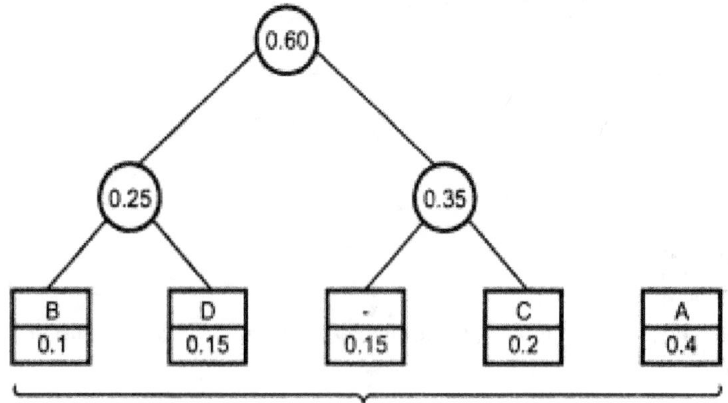



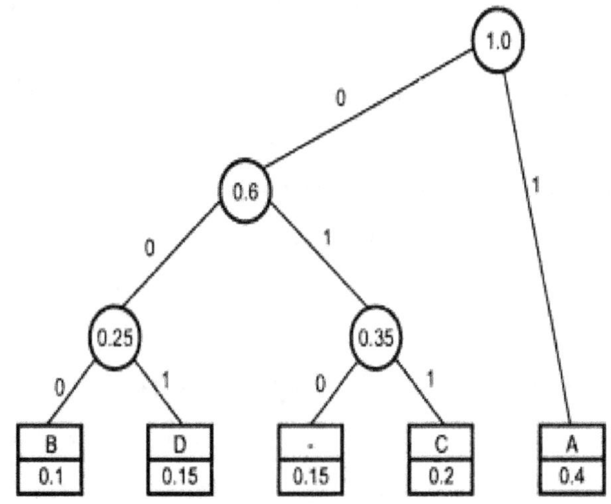



The left branch is assigned 0 and right branch is assigned with 1. Hence coding of each character is

| A | B | C | D | - |
|---|-----|-----|-----|-----|
| 1 | 000 | 011 | 001 | 010 |

a.   ABACABAD can be encoded as 1000101110001001.

b.   The decoding of 100010111001010 is ABACAD.

### 1. Define greedy concept

Greedy technique constructs a solution to an optimization problem by piece by piece through a sequence of choice that are:

- Feasible
- Locally optimal
- Irrevocable

For some problems, yields an optimal solution for every instance. For most, does not but can be useful for fast approximations.

### 2. Define container loading

A large ship is to be loaded with cargo. The cargo is containerized and all containers are the same size. Different containers may have different weights. $w_i$ be the weight of the $i^{th}$ container $1 \leq i \leq n$.

The cargo capacity is C. Based on the greedy concept load the ship with the maximum number of containers.

### 3. What is the complexity of container loading?

Complexity of an algorithm in terms of time and space.

#### Space Complexity

Space for weight of n containers stored in an array c[ ] = n locations

Space for indication of container loading stored in an array x[ ] = n locations

Capacity of cargo c = 1 location

Numbers of containers 'n' = 1 location

Control variable 'i' = 1 location

Therefore, total space required = 2n+ 3

#### Time Complexity

Sorting the container increasing order of their weight using merge sort = O(log n)

Algorithm for loading of container = O(n)

Therefore, time complexity = O(n log n)

## 4. *Define complexity of knapsack problem*

### *Space Complexity*

Space for profit array = n locations

Space for weight array = n locations

Space for solution array = n locations

Capacity of knapsack m = 1 location

Numbers of objects 'n' = 1 location

Control variable 'i' = 1 location

Therefore, total space required = 3(n + 1)

### *Time Complexity*

Sorting the order = O( n)

Algorithm for filling the knapsack = O(n)

Therefore, time complexity = O(n )

## 5. *Define knapsack problem*

We are given n objects and a knapsack or bag. Object i has a weight $w_i$ and the knapsack has a capacity m. if a fraction $x_i$, $(0 \leq x_i \leq 1)$ of object 'i' is placed into the knapsack, then a profit $p_i x_i$ is earned.

The objective is to obtain a filling of the knapsack that maximizes the total profit earned.

# UNIT 4

## Dynamic Programming

Dynamic Programming: General Method – Multistage Graphs – All-Pair shortest paths – Optimal binary search trees – 0/1 Knapsack – Travelling salesperson problem.

### 4.1. Dynamic Programming

Dynamic Programming is a technique for solving problems with overlapping sub problems. The smaller sub problems are solved only once and recording the results in a table from which the solution to the original problem is obtained.

### 4.2. Multistage Graphs

*Concept*

The multistage graph is to find a minimum cost path from source 's' to sink 't' i.e destination.

*Problem Description*

- A multistage graph $G=(V, E)$ is a directed graph in which the vertices are partitioned into $k > =2$ disjoint sets $V_i$, $[1 \leq I \leq k]$
- If $(u, v)$ is an edge in E, then $U \varepsilon V_i$ and $V \varepsilon V_{i+1}$ for some $i$, $[1 \leq I \leq k]$
- The sets $V_1$ and $V_K$ are such that $|V_1| = |V_K| = 1$.
- The vertex 's' is the source and 't' is the sink.
- Let $c(i, j)$ be the cost of edge $(i, j)$
- The cost of a path from 's' to 't' is the sum of the cost of the edges on the path.
- Each set $V_i$ defines a stag in the graph.
- Every path from S to t starts in stage 1 goes to stage 2, Then to stage 3 then to stage 4 and so on and eventually terminates at stage k.

*Procedure for Multistage Problems*

- Find path from s to t stage by stage.
- Every s to t path is the result of a sequence of k-2 decisions.
- The $i^{th}$ decision involves determining which vertex in $V_{i+1}$, $1 \leq i \leq k-2$ is to be on the path.
- $P(i, j)$ be a minimum cost path from vertex j in $V_i$ to vertex t.
- Cost $(i, j)$ be the cost of the path.

- Find cost of path using the formula.

$$\text{Cost}(i, j) = \min\{c(j, l) + \text{cost}(i+1, l)\}$$
$$l \in V_{i+1}, \ (j, l) \in E$$

- Shortest distance between source 's' and sink 't' using following formula.

  Cost (1, s) by first computing

$$\text{Cost}(k-2, j) \text{ for all } j \in V_{K-2}$$
$$\text{Cost}(k-3, j) \text{ for all } j \in V_{K-3}$$
$$\text{Cost}(1, s)$$

## 4.2.1. *Example for Multistage Graph*

Find the shortest distance between source 's' and sink 't'.

Using 5 stage graph.

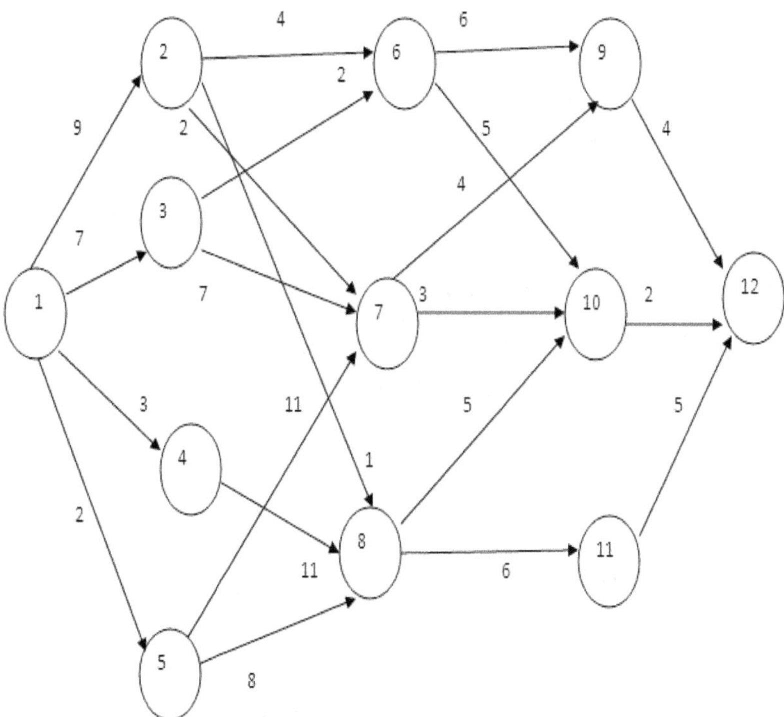

1.  Compute cost (k—2, j) for all j ε V $_{K\_2}$.K= 5, because it is 5 stage graph.

III stage contains 6, 7 & 8 i.e., 3 nodes.

Cost (i, j) = min{ c,(j,l)+cost (i+1,l)}

Cost (3, 6)  =min {6+cost (4, 9), 5+ cost (4, 10)}

= min {6+4, 5+2}

= min {10, 7}

=7

Cost (3, 7) =min {c (j, 1) +cost (i+1, 1)}

= min {4+cost (4, 9), 3+ cost (4, 10)}

=min {4+4, 3+2}

=min {8, 5}

=5

Cost (3, 8) = min {c (j, l) + cost (i+1, l)}

=min {5+ cost (4. 10), 6+ cost (4, 11)}

=min {5+2.6+5}

=min {7, 11}

=7

2.  Compute cost (k—3, j) for all j ε $V_{K\_3}$.

II stage contains 2, 3, 4 & 5 nodes.

Cost (2, 2) =min {4+cost (3, 6),2 + cost (3,7) 1+cost (3.8)}

= min {(4+7), (2+5), (1+7)}

= min {11, 7, 8}

=7

Cost (2, 3) = min {2 + cost (3, 6), 7+ cost (3, 7)}

=min {( 2+7), (7+5)}

=min {9, 12}

=9

Cost (2, 4) = min {11+cost (3,8)}

      =min {11+7}

      =18

Cost (2, 5) = min {11 + cost (3, 7), 8 + cost (3, 8)}

      =min {(11+5),(8+7)}

      =min {16, 15}

      =15

3.   Compute cost (1, s)

I stage contains 1 node

Cost (1, 1) = min {9+cost (2, 2) 7+cost (2, 3),3+ cost (2, 4) 2 + cost (2, 5)}

      = min (9+7, 7+9, 3+18, 2+15}

      = min {16, 16, 21, 17}

      =16

A minimum cost from's' to't' path=16

The path from's' to't' in indicated by broken edge.

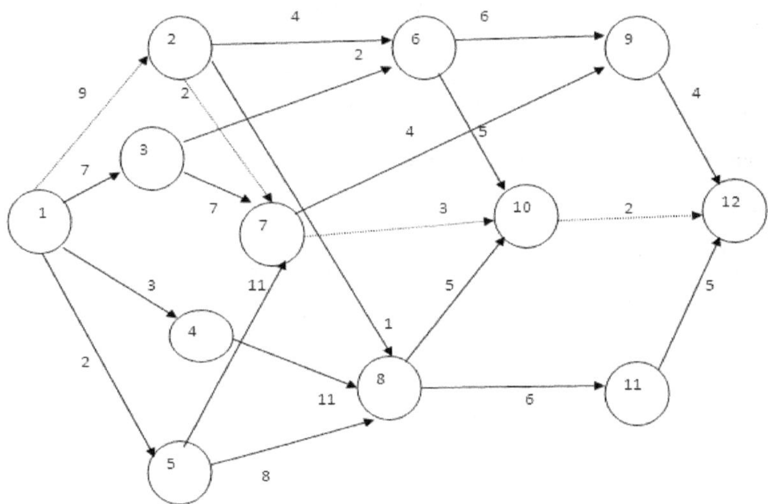

Fig. 4.1: Shortest Path from's' to't' Using in Multistage Graph

### 4.2.2. *Example*

Find the shortest path between source's' and sink't' using multistage graph.

Solution:

Find the shortest path between source's' and sink't' using 5 stage graph.

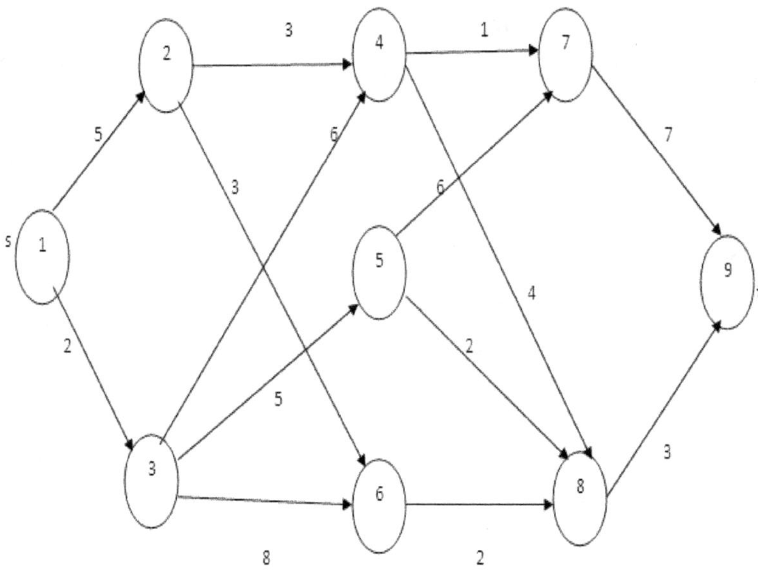


1. First compute cost (k—2, j) for all j ∈ $V_{K-2}$, k = 5 because it is 5 stage graph.

   III stage contains 3 nodes such as 4, 5 & 6.

   Cost (i,j)  = min {c (i, l) + cost (i+1, l)}

      Cost (3, 4) = min { 1 + cost (4, 7), 4 + cost (4, 8)}

               = min { (1+7), (4+3)}

               =min {8,7}

               =7

      Cost (3,5) = min {c (j. 1) + cost (i+1, l)}

            =min { 6 + cost (4, 7), 2 + cost (4, 8)}

            = min { (6+7), (2+3)}

$$=\min \{13,5\}$$

$$=5$$

$$\text{Cost } (3,6) = \min\{c(j,l)+cost(i+1,l)\}$$

$$= \min \{6+cost (4, 7), 2+cost (4, 8)\}$$

$$= \min \{(6+7), (2+3)\}$$

$$= \min \{13, 5)$$

$$=5$$

2. Compute cost $(k\text{-}3,j)$ for all $j\epsilon V_{k\text{-}3}$ , Where k=5

   II stage contains 2 nodes such as 2 and 3.

$$\text{Cost}(2,2)=\min \{c(j,l)+cost(i+1,l)\}$$

$$=\min\{3+ cost (3, 4), 3 + cost (3, 6)\}$$

$$= mm \{(3+7), (3+5)\}$$

$$=\min \{10,8\}$$

$$=8$$

$$\text{Cost}(2,3)= mm \{c j, 1) + cost (i+1, 1))$$

$$= \min\{6 + cost (3, 4), 5+cost (3. 5), 8+ cost (3, 6)\}$$

$$= \min \{(6+7), (5+5), (8+5)\}$$

$$= \min \{13, 10, 13\}$$

$$=10$$

3. Compute cost $(1, s)$

   I stage contains only one node 1.

$$\text{Cost } (1,1)=\min \{5 + cost (2, 2), 2+ cost (2, 3)\}$$

$$=\min \{(5+8),(2+ 10)\},\min \{13, 12\}$$

$$=12$$

A minimum cost from 's' for to 't' is 12 .

The path from s to t is indicated by broken edges.

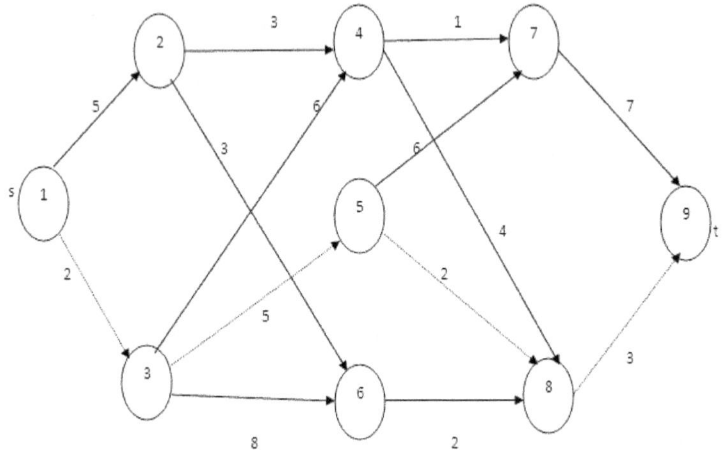



Fig. 4.2: Shortest Path from 'S' to t Using 5 Stage Graph

Algorithm for multistage graph using forward approach

Void FGraph (Graph G, int k, int n, int p [ ])

{//the input is a k stage graph G = (V, E)

With n vertices.

// indexed in order of stages.

// E is a set of edges and c [i, j] is the cost of (i,j)

// P [i : k] in a minimum cost path vertex

{

    Cost [n] = 0.0; //cost of vertex n is zero

    for (j= n-1; j > = 1;j--)

{

    // compute cost [j]

    //let r be a vertex such that (j, r) is an edge of G and

    // c [j, r] + cost [r] is minimum

    Cost [j] = c [j, r] + cost [r];

    d [j] =r;}

// Find a minimum cost path

P [1] =1;

P [k] =n;

for (j =2;j <=k—1;j+1)

P[j] =d [P [j—1]];

} }

## *Multistage Graph Using Backward Approach*

- Multistage can be solved using backward graph approach.
- Let bp (i, j) a minimum cost path from vertex s to a j in $V_i$
- bcost (i,j) be the cost of bp (i,j).

  Shortest path from source's' to sink t' using backward approach.

$$bcost(i,j)= min\{bcost((i-j,l)+c(l,j)\}$$
$$l \in V_{i-1}, \quad (l,j) \in E$$

- bcost(2,j)=c(1,j)    if(1,j)$\in$ E

  bcost (2,j) =$\alpha$ if(1, j) $\in$ E

Find shortest path from source's' to sink't' for the following graph using backward approach.

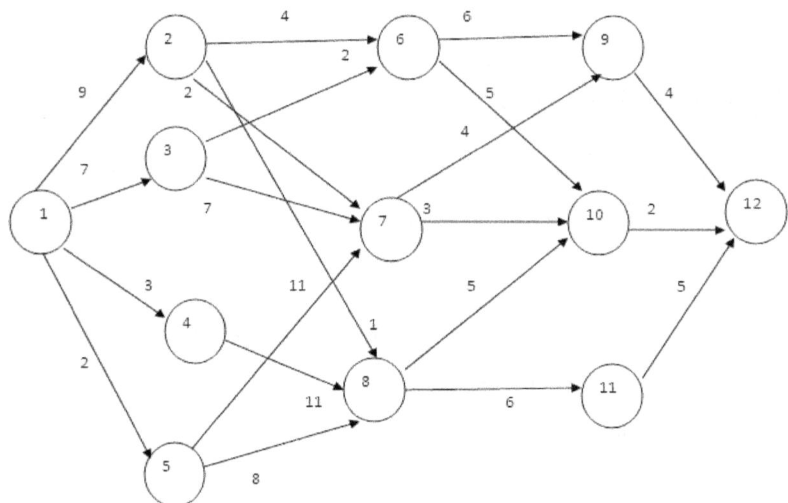

1. Compute bcost for i=2.

bcost $(2, 2)$ =min{c(1,2)}

= 9

bcost $(2, 3)$ =min{c(1,3)}

= 7

bcost $(2, 4)$ =min{c(1,4)}

= 3

bcost $(2, 5)$ =min{c(1,5)}

= 2

2. Compute bcost for i = 3.

bcost $(3, 6)$ = min {bcost (2,2)+c(2,6), bcost (2,3)+ c (3,6) }

= min {(9+4), (7+2)}

=min{13,9}

= 9

bcost $(3, 7)$ = min {bcost (2,2) + c (2,7), bcost (2, 3) + c (3, 7), bcost(2, 5) (5, 7)}

= min { (9+2), (7+7). (2+11)}

= min { 11, 14, 13}

=11

bcost $(3, 8)$ = min {bcost (2, 2) + c (2, 8), bcost (2, 4) + C (4. 8). bcost (2.5) +c(5,8)}

= min {(9+1), (3+1 1), (2+8)}

= min {10.14, 10}

= 10

3. Compute bcost for i=4

bcost $(4, 9)$ = min { bcost (3, 6) + C (6, 9), bcost (3, 7) + c (7, 9)}

= min { (9+6), (11+5)}

=min {15. 16}

= 15

bcost(4,10) = min { bcost (3, 6) + c (6, 10),bcost(3,7)+c(7,10),bcost (3, 8) + c (8, 10)}

=min {(9+5), (11+3), (10+5))

= min {14, 14, 15)

= 14

bcost(4, 11)=min { bcost (3, 8) + c (8,11)}

=min{10+6}

=16

4. Compute bcost for i=5

bcost (5, 12)=min {bcost (4, 9) + c (9, 12),bcost (4. 10) + c (10, 12),bcost(4, 11)+c(11,12)}

= min {(15+4), (14+2) (16+5)}

= min {19, 16, 21}

= 16

Cost of the path from source's' to 't'= 16

The broken edge indicate the shortest path from source's' to sink 't'.

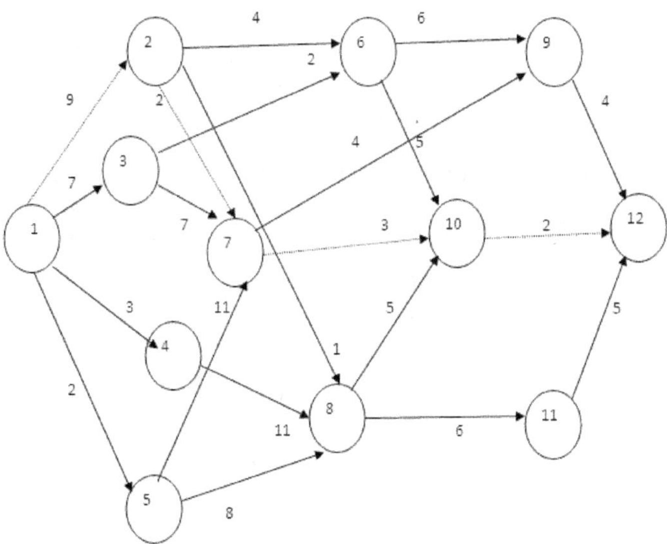

Shortest path from source's' to sink 't' using backward approach.

Find shortest path form source 's' to sink 't' for the following graph using backward approach.

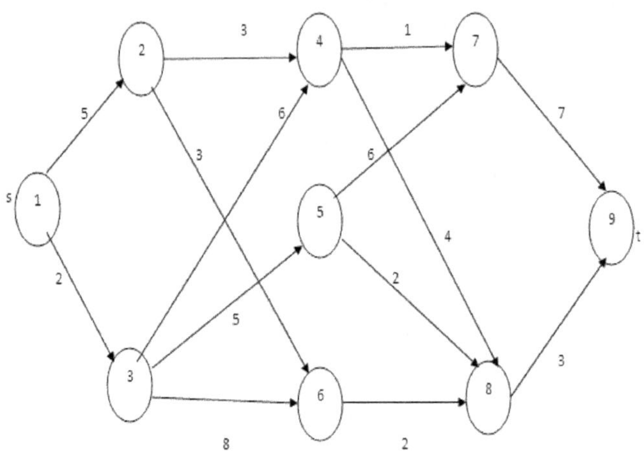

1.  Compute bcost for i = 2

    bcost (2, 2)   = c (1, 2)

                =5

    bcost(2,3)    = c(1,3)

                =2

2.  Compute bcost for i =3

    bcost (3, 4) = min { bcost (2. 2) + c ( 2. 4), bcost (2, 3) + c (3, 4)}

          = min {(5+3), (2+6))

          = 8

    bcost (3, 5) = min {bcost (2, 3) + c (3, 5)}

          =min{2+5}

          =7

    bcost (3,6)  =min { bcost(2,2)+c(2,6),bcost(2,3)+c(3,6)}

          = min {(5+3), (2+8)}

          = min {8, 10)

          = 8

3. Compute bcost for i=4

bcost (4, 7)  = min { bcost (3, 4) + c (4, 7), bcost ( 3, 5) + c ( 5, 7) bcost (3, 6) + c (6, 7)}

=min {(8+1), (7+6), (8+6)}

= min {9, 13, 14}

=9

bcost (4, 8)  = min { bcost (3, 4) + c (4, 8), bcost (3, 5) + c (5, 8), bcost (3, 6) + c (6, 8)}

= min {(8+4), (7+2) ,(8+2)}

=min {12, 9, 10}

=9

4. Compute bcost for i = 5

bcost (5, 9) = min { bcost (4, 7) + c (7, 9), bcost (4, 8) + c (8. 9)}

= min {(9+7),(9+3)}

= min {16, 12}

= 12

Shortest path from source 's' to sink 't' = 12

Shortest path form sources' to sink't' indicated by broken edge.

Edges (8, 9), (5. 8), (3, 5), (1, 3) shown with broken lines.

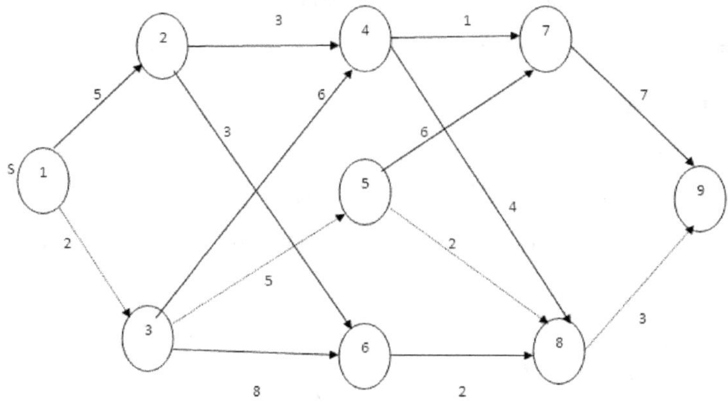



Shortest path from source 'S' to sink 't' using backward approach.

### *Algorithm for Multistage Graph Using Backward Approach*

```
void BGraph (Graph G, int k, int n, int p [ ])

    {  bcost [1] = 0.0;

    // cost of vertex 1 is zero.

    for (j=2; j<n; j ++)

    {  // compute bcost [j]

    // Let r be such that (r, j) is an edge

    // of G and bcost [r] + c [r, j] is minimum

    bcost [j]= bcost [r]+ c [r,j];

    d[j]=r;

    // Find a minimum cost path

    P [1] =1; P[k] =n;

    for(j=k-1;j>2;j--)

    P[j]=d[p[j+1]];

}
```

Complexity of multistage graph for both forward and backward approach.

### *Time Complexity*

Finding the minimum cost for each and every stage $=\Theta (|V| + |E|)$

Shortest path from source s to sink t —> $\Theta$ (k)

### *Space Complexity*

| | |
|---|---|
| Storage space for cost array, cost [ ] | =n location |
| Storage space for minimum cost path P [ ] | = n location |
| Storage space for decision array d [1] | = n location |
| Storage space for stage k | =1 |
| Storage space for variable 'n' | =1 |
| Control variable j | =i |
| Total storage space 3n+3 | = 3 (n+ 1) j |

## 4.3. All Pairs Shortest Path

*Concept*

Given a weighted connected graph, the all pair shortest path problem is used to find the distance from each vertex to all other vertices.

The graph may be either directed or undirected graph.

*Procedure for All Pair Shortest Path Problem*

- Let $G = (V, E)$ is a directed graph with n vertices.
- Let cost be a cost adjacency matrix for G such that cost(i. i) =0,

$$1 \leq i \leq n$$

- Cost (i,j) is the length of edge (i ,j)  if< i, j> $\varepsilon$ E (G)
- Cost (i, j) = $\alpha$ if i $\neq$ j and (i, j) $\varepsilon$ $\not{E}$ (G)
- Examine a shortest path 'i' to 'j' if i $\neq$ j
- This path originates at vertex 'i' and goes through some intermediate vertices and terminates at vertex j.
- It compute the distance matrix of a weighted graph with n vertices through a series of n by n matrices.
- The series of n by n matrices are $A^{(0)}$,........$A^{(k-1)}$ A $^K$....$A^{(n)}$
- The element Aij(k) in the ith row and kth column of matrix Ak (k =0, 1, . . .n) is equal to the length of the shortest path among all paths from $i^{th}$ vertex to the $j^{th}$ vertex with each intermediate vertex, is any numbered not higher than k.
- The initial matrix $A^{(0)}$ does not allow any intermediate vertices in its path which is nothing but the weight matrix of the graph.
- The final matrix $A^{(n)}$contains the length of the shortest paths among all paths that use all n vertices as intermediate.
- All the elements of each matrix $A^k$ is computed from its predecessor $A^{k-1}$ in the series

    $A^{(0)}$,....$A^{(k-1)}$ $A^{(k)}$...$A^{(n)}$

- $Aij^{(k)}$ is equal to the length of the shortest path among all the paths from vertex to $i^{th}$ vertex to $j^{th}$ vertex with their intermediate vertices not higher than k.
- The path is given by

    $V_i$, a list of intermediate vertices each, $V_j$ numbered not higher than k,$V_j$

- All paths are partitioned into 2 disjoint subsets.

    1. First subset contains paths that do not use $k^{th}$ vertex as intermediate.

    2. Second subset contains path that use kth vertex as intermediate.

- The paths of the first subset have their intermediate vertices numbered higher than k-1. then the shortest length is $Aij^{(k-1)}$

- The path of the second subset is given by

$$V_i, \text{vertices numbered} \leq k-1, V_k \quad \text{Vertices numbered} \leq k-1, V_j$$

- That is, each path in the second subset is made up of a path from $V_i$ to $V_k$ with each intermediate vertex numbered not higher than k-1 & a path from $V_k$ to Vj with each intermediate vertex numbered not higher than k-1 & a path from $V_k$ to $V_j$ with each intermediate vertex numbered not higher than k-1.

- Path from $V_i$ to $V_k$ with intermediate, vertex not more than k -1.

$$A^{k-1}(i,k)$$

- Path from $V_k$ to $V_j$ with intermediate vertex not more than k.

$$A^{k-1}(k,j)$$

- Length of shortest path = $\boxed{A^{k-1}(i,k) + A^{k-1}(k,j)}$

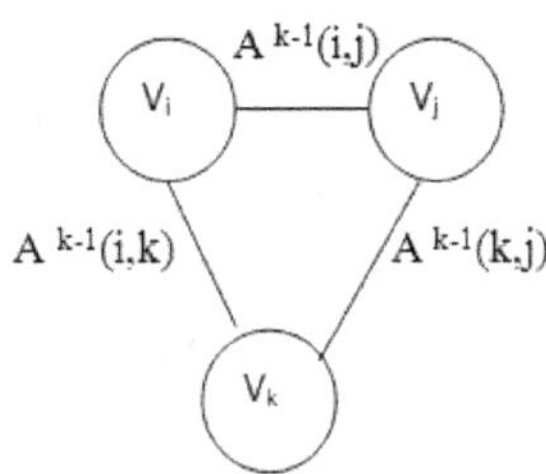


Fig. 4.3: All Pair Shortest Path Problem

### Length of the Shortest Path

By taking the length of the shortest paths in both subsets, the length shortest path is given as

$$A^k(i,j) = \min\{A^{k-1}(i,j), A^{k-1}(i,k) + A^{k-1}(k,j)\} \quad k \geq 1$$

$$A(i,j) = W(i,j) \quad W(i,j) = \text{Weight matrix}$$

## *Examples for All pair shortest path problem*

### *Example 1: Find all pair shortest path for the following graph*

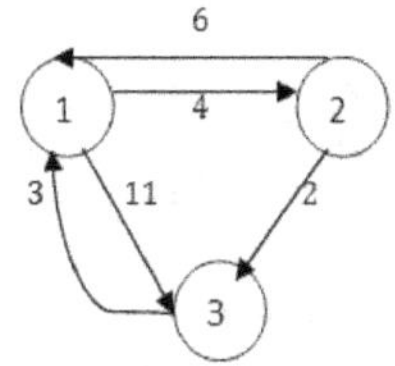


1.  Find weight matrix of a graph is

$$W = A^{(0)} =$$

|   | 1 | 2 | 3  |
|---|---|---|----|
| 1 | 0 | 4 | 11 |
| 2 | 6 | 0 | 2  |
| 3 | 3 | α | 0  |

Length of the shortest path with no intermediate vertices is obtained.

2.  The boxed row and column is used to generate the matrix $A^{(1)}$

$$
\begin{array}{c}
1 \\
2 \\
3
\end{array}
\left[
\begin{array}{ccc}
0 & 4 & 11 \\
6 & 0 & 2 \\
3 & α & 0
\end{array}
\right]
$$

3.  Length of the shortest path with intermediate vertices numbered not higher than 1.

    one new $3 \longrightarrow 2 = 3 \longrightarrow 1 \longrightarrow 2$ path is obtained.

    $$= 3+4 \quad = 7.$$

$$
A^{(1)} =
\begin{array}{c}
\phantom{0} \\
1 \\
2 \\
3
\end{array}
\begin{array}{ccc}
1 & 2 & 3 \\
\left[\begin{array}{ccc}
0 & 4 & 11 \\
6 & 0 & 2 \\
3 & 7 & 0
\end{array}\right]
\end{array}
$$

4.  The boxed row and column in $A^{(1)}$ is used to generate the elements of $A^{(2)}$.

$$
A^{(1)} =
\begin{array}{c}
\phantom{0} \\
1 \\
2 \\
3
\end{array}
\begin{array}{ccc}
1 & 2 & 3 \\
\left[\begin{array}{ccc}
0 & 4 & 11 \\
6 & 0 & 2 \\
3 & 7 & 0
\end{array}\right]
\end{array}
$$

5. Length of the shortest path with intermediate vertices numbered not higher than 2 . The new path $1 \to 2 \to 3 = 4+2 = 6$ is obtained.

$$A^{(2)} = \begin{array}{c@{}c} & \begin{array}{ccc} 1 & 2 & 3 \end{array} \\ \begin{array}{c} 1 \\ 2 \\ 3 \end{array} & \left[\begin{array}{ccc} 0 & 4 & 6 \\ 6 & 0 & 2 \\ 3 & 7 & 0 \end{array}\right] \end{array}$$

6. The boxed row and column in $A^{(1)}$ is used to generate the elements of next matrix $A^{(3)}$.

$$A^{(2)} = \begin{array}{c@{}c} & \begin{array}{ccc} 1 & 2 & 3 \end{array} \\ \begin{array}{c} 1 \\ 2 \\ 3 \end{array} & \left[\begin{array}{ccc} 0 & 4 & \boxed{6} \\ 6 & 0 & 2 \\ \boxed{3} & \boxed{7} & 0 \end{array}\right] \end{array}$$

7. Lengths of the shortest path with intermediate numbered not higher than 3.The new path $2 \to 3 \to 1 = 2+3 = 5$ is obtained.

$$A^{(3)} = \begin{array}{c@{}c} & \begin{array}{ccc} 1 & 2 & 3 \end{array} \\ \begin{array}{c} 1 \\ 2 \\ 3 \end{array} & \left[\begin{array}{ccc} 0 & 4 & 6 \\ 5 & 0 & 2 \\ 3 & 7 & 0 \end{array}\right] \end{array}$$

***Example 2: Find all pair shortest path for the following graph***

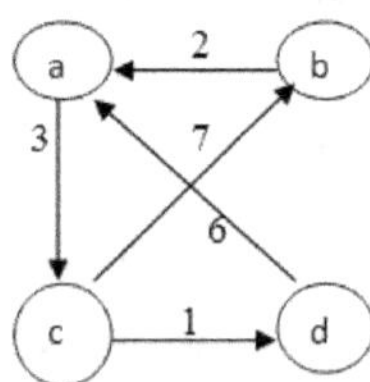


1. Find weight matrix of a graph is

$$W = A^{(0)} = \begin{pmatrix} 0 & \alpha & 3 & \alpha \\ 2 & 0 & \alpha & \alpha \\ \alpha & 7 & 0 & 1 \\ 6 & \alpha & \alpha & 0 \end{pmatrix}$$

A length of the shortest path with no intermediate vertices is obtained.

2. The boxed row and column is used to generate the matrix A $^{(1)}$

$$A^{(0)} = \begin{array}{c|cccc} & a & b & c & d \\ \hline a & 0 & \alpha & 3 & \alpha \\ b & 2 & 0 & \alpha & \alpha \\ c & \alpha & 7 & 0 & 1 \\ d & 6 & \alpha & \alpha & 0 \end{array}$$

3. Length of the shortest paths with intermediate vertices numbered not higher than 1 just a is found. Two new shortest paths are obtained. They are

1. b $\xrightarrow{2}$ a $\xrightarrow{3}$ c length is 5.

2. d $\xrightarrow{6}$ a $\xrightarrow{3}$ c length is 9.

$$A(1) = \begin{pmatrix} 0 & \alpha & 3 & \alpha \\ 2 & 0 & 5 & \alpha \\ \alpha & 7 & 0 & 1 \\ 6 & \alpha & 9 & 0 \end{pmatrix}$$

4. The boxed row and column in A $^{(1)}$ is used to generate the elements of A $^{(2)}$.

$$A^{(1)} = \begin{array}{c|cccc} & a & b & c & d \\ \hline a & 0 & \alpha & 3 & \alpha \\ b & 2 & 0 & 5 & \alpha \\ c & \alpha & 7 & 0 & 1 \\ d & 6 & \alpha & \alpha & 0 \end{array}$$

5. Length of the shortest paths with intermediate vertices numbered not higher than 2 i.e., a and b is found.

One new shortest path c $\xrightarrow{7}$ b $\xrightarrow{2}$ a length is 9.

$$A^{(2)} = \begin{array}{c|cccc} & a & b & c & d \\ \hline a & 0 & \alpha & 3 & \alpha \\ b & 2 & 0 & 5 & \alpha \\ c & 9 & 7 & 0 & 1 \\ d & 6 & \alpha & 9 & 0 \end{array}$$

6.  The boxed row and column in $A^{(2)}$ is used to generate the elements of next matrix A(3)

$$
A^{(2)} = 
\begin{array}{c|cccc}
 & a & b & c & d \\
\hline
a & 0 & \alpha & \boxed{3} & \alpha \\
b & 2 & 0 & \boxed{5} & \alpha \\
c & \boxed{9} & \boxed{7} & \boxed{0} & \boxed{1} \\
d & 6 & \alpha & \boxed{9} & 0 \\
\end{array}
$$

7.  The length of the shortest path with intermediate vertices numbered not higher than 3. i.e., b and c.

4 new paths

$$\overset{3}{\phantom{a}}\quad\overset{7}{\phantom{c}}$$
1. a ---> c ---->          b=length is 10

$$\overset{3}{\phantom{a}}\quad\overset{1}{\phantom{c}}$$
2. a ----> c---->          d=length is 4

$$\overset{2}{\phantom{b}}\quad\overset{3}{\phantom{a}}\quad\overset{1}{\phantom{c}}$$
3. b ----->a --- >c ---- >    d=length is 6

$$\overset{6}{\phantom{d}}\quad\overset{3}{\phantom{a}}\quad\overset{7}{\phantom{c}}$$
4. d ---- > a ----> c ---- >  b = length is 16

$$
A^{(3)} = 
\begin{array}{c|cccc}
 & a & b & c & d \\
\hline
a & 0 & 10 & 3 & 4 \\
b & 2 & 0 & 5 & 6 \\
c & 9 & 7 & 0 & 1 \\
d & 6 & 16 & 9 & 0 \\
\end{array}
$$

8.  The boxed row and column in A (3) is used to generate the elements of matrix A(4).

$$
A^{(3)} = 
\begin{array}{c|cccc}
 & a & b & c & d \\
\hline
a & 0 & 10 & 3 & \boxed{4} \\
b & 2 & 0 & 5 & \boxed{6} \\
c & 9 & 7 & 0 & \boxed{1} \\
d & \boxed{6} & \boxed{16} & \boxed{9} & \boxed{0} \\
\end{array}
$$

9.  The length of the shortest path with intermediate vertices numbered not greater than 4 i.e., (a, b, c & d) is found.

One new shortest path c ---> d ---->a = **7**

## Algorithm for All Pair Shortest Path

Void allpaths(float cost[] [],int size, int n, float A[] [])

//cost [n] [n] in the cost of adjacency matrix of a graph with n vertices

// A [i] [j]is the cost of a shortest path from vertex 'i' to vertex 'j'.

// cost [i][j] =0.0 for $1 \leq i \leq n$.

{

for (i=1;i<=n;i++)

for (j=1;j<=n;j++)

//copy cost into an A array

A [i] [j] = cost [i] [j];

for (k= 1;k<=n;k++)

for (i=1;i<n;i++)

for (j= 1;j<=n;j++)

A [i] [j] = min (A [i] [j], A [i] [k] + A [k] [i])

}

## Complexity of All Pair Shortest Path Problem

Complexity of an algorithm depends on space and time complexity

## Space Complexity

| | |
|---|---|
| Storage space for cost array c [n] [n] | $= n^2$ location |
| Storage space for storing intermediate results A [n] [n] | $= n^2$ location |
| Storage space for n | = 1 location |
| Storage space for control variable i, j, k | = 3 location |

Therefore Total space $\boxed{2n^2+4}$

## Time Complexity

For finding all pair shortest path, algorithm uses 3 for loops

So time complexity is $\boxed{O(n^3)}$

### Optimal Binary Search Tree

### Concept

Dynamic programming is used for constructing an optimal binary search tree for a given set of keys and known probabilities. If probabilities of searching for elements of a set are known, it is natural have an optimal binary search tree for which the average number of comparisons in a search is the smallest possible.

**Example 1**: Possible binary search tree for the following identifiers (do, for, while, int, if).

a. We can create different binary search trees for the same identifier set to have different performance characteristics.

b. In the worst case requires 4 comparisons. It takes 1,2,2,3 & 4 comparison to find the identifiers for, do, while, int, if. Thus average number of comparisons

$$= \frac{1+2+2+3+4}{5} = \frac{12}{5}$$

In the worst case requires 3 comparisons. It takes 1, 2, 2, 3, 3 comparison to find the identifiers for, do, while, int, if

Average no of comparisons

$$= \frac{1+2+2+3+4}{5} = \frac{12}{5}$$

### General Procedure to Find Cost of Binary Tree

- To obtain a cost function for binary search tree, it is useful to add external node in place of every empty sub tree.
- If a binary search tree represents n identifiers then there will be exactly (n) internal nodes and (n + 1) external nodes.
- Every internal node represents a point where successful search may terminate.
- Every external node represents a point where unsuccessful search may terminate.

### Successful Search

- Let us assume that the given set of identifiers is $\{a_2, a_2, \ldots\ldots An\}$ with $a_1 < a_2 < a_n$.
- Let P (i) be the probability for search $a_i$.
- The successful search terminates at internal node.

- The cost contribution for successful search for node

$$a_i = \boxed{P(i) * \text{level}(a_i)}$$

## Unsuccessful Search

- Let $q(i)$ be the probability for unsuccessful search of the node $a_i$.
- The unsuccessful search terminates at external node
- The identifiers not in the binary search tree can be partitioned into $n + I$ equivalence classes. $E_i$, $0 \leq i \leq n$.
- $E_0$ contains all identifiers x such that $x < a_1$.
- The class $E_i$ contains all identifiers x such that $a_i < x < a_i + 1$, $1 \leq i \leq n$.
- The class $E_n$ contains all identifiers x, $x > a_n$.
- The identifiers in different $E_i$, the search terminates at different external node.
- The cost contribution for unsuccessful search for node $a_i$.

$$\boxed{q(i)*(\text{Level}(E_i)-1)}$$

## Cost of Binary Search Tree

The cost of binary tree can be calculated using following formula

$$\boxed{\sum_{1 \leq i \leq n} P(i)*\text{level}(a_i) + \sum_{0 \leq i \leq n} q(i)*(\text{level}(E_i)-1)}$$

## Example

The possible binary search trees for the identifiers set $(a_1, a_2, a_3) = (do, While, If)$.

The probability for successful search

$$P(1) = .5, P(2) = .1, P(3) = 0.05$$

The probability for unsuccessful search

$$q(0) = .15, q(1) = .1, q(2) = .05, q(3) = .05$$

1. Compute cost for binary search tree

    Successful search for the identifier (do, if, while)

    Successful search for 'do'    $= 3 * 0.5 = 1.5$

    Successful search for 'if'    $= 2*0.1 = 0.2$

    Successful search for 'while' $= 1 * 0.05 = 0.05 = 0.05$

$$\sum_{1 \le i \le n} P(i) * level(a_i) = 1.5+0.2+0.05 = 1.75$$

Unsuccessful search for the identifier (do, if, while)

Unsuccessful search for 'do'      = 3 x 0.15

Unsuccessful search for 'if'      = 3 * 0.1

Unsuccessful search for 'while'   = 2 * 0.05

$$\sum_{0 \le i \le n} q(i) * (level(E_1)....1) \quad = 0.05 + .10 + .3 + 0.45$$

$$= 0.90$$

Total cost for binary search tree = 1.75 + 0.90

$$= 2.65$$

2.   Compute cost for binary search tree.

## Successful Search

Successful search for 'if'      = 1*0.1 = 0.10

Successful search for 'do'      = 2*0.5 = 1.0

Successful search for 'while'   = 2* 0.05 = 0.10

$$\sum P(i) * (level(a_i) \quad = 0.10 + 1.0 + 0.10$$

$$= 1.20$$

## Unsuccessful Search

Unsuccessful search for 'if'      = 2*.1 = .2

Unsuccessful search for 'do'      = 2*0.15 = .3

Unsuccessful search for 'while'   = 2*0.05 = .1

$$\sum_{1 \le i \le n} (q_i * (level(E_i) - 1)) \quad = 0.1 + 0.2 + 0.3 + 0.1$$

$$= 0.70$$

Total cost for binary search tree = 1.20 + 0.70

$$= 1.90$$

3. Compute cost for binary search tree.

### Successful Search

| | |
|---|---|
| Successful search for 'do' | $=1*.5=0.5$ |
| Successful search for 'if' | $=2*.1=0.2$ |
| Successful search for 'while' | $=3*0.05=0.15$ |
| Total search cost for all identifier | $=0.5+0.2+0.15$ |
| | $=0.85$ |

### Unsuccessful Search

| | |
|---|---|
| Unsuccessful search for 'do' | $= 1 * .15 = .15$ |
| Unsuccessful search for 'if' | $= 3*1 = .3$ |
| Unsuccessful search for 'while' | $= 3 * .05 = .15$ |

Total search cost for unsuccessful search = $\sum q(i)*(level(E_i)-1)$

$$0 \leq i \leq n$$

$$= .15+.3+.15+0.05 = 0.65$$

| | |
|---|---|
| Total cost for binary search tree | $= (0.85+0.65)$ |
| | $= 1.50$ |

4. Compute cost for binary search tree.

### Successful Search

| | |
|---|---|
| Successful search for 'while' | $=1*0.05 = 0.05$ |
| Successful search for 'do' | $=2 * .5 = 1.0$ |
| Successful search for 'if' | $=3 *.1 =0.3$ |
| Total successful search | $=1.35$ |

### Unsuccessful Search

| | |
|---|---|
| Unsuccessful search for 'while' | $=1*0.05 = 0.05$ |
| Unsuccessful search for 'do' | $=2 *0.15=0.30$ |
| Unsuccessful search for 'if' | $=3 *.1 =0.3$ |

| Total Unsuccessful search | $= \sum q(i)*(\text{level }(E_i)-1)$ |
|---|---|

$$o \leq i \leq n$$

$$= 0.05 + 0.30 + 0.3 + 0.05 = 0.70$$

| Total cost for binary search tree | $=1.35+0.80$ |
|---|---|

$$=2.05$$

5.  Compute cost for binary search tree .

| Successful search for do' | $=1*.5=0.5$ |
|---|---|
| Successful search for 'while' | $=2 * 0.05 \; 0.1$ |
| Successful search for 'if' | $=3*.3=0.3$ |
| Total search | $=0.5 + 0.1+ 0.3$ |
| | $=0.9$ |

## *Unsuccessful Search*

| Unsuccessful search for 'do' | $=.15$ |
|---|---|
| Unsuccessful search for 'while' | $=.15$ |
| Unsuccessful search for 'if' | $=.30$ |
| Total unsuccessful search | $= \sum q(i)*(\text{level }(E_i)-1) = .15+.15+.30+0.05 = 0.65$ |

$$0 \leq i \leq n$$

| Total search cost | $= 0.9 + 0.65 = 1.55$ |
|---|---|

## *Procedure to Find the Cost of Binary Search Tree Using Dynamic Programming*

- Construction of optimal binary search tree as the result of sequence of decisions.
- A possible approach to this would be to make a decision as to which of the $a_i$'s should be assigned to the root node of the tree.
- If we choose $a_k$, then it is clear that the internal nodes for $a_1$, $a_2$, $a_3$,..$a_{k-1}$ as well as the external nodes for the classes $E_0$, $E_1$, $E_2$.....$E_{k-1}$ will be lie in the left subtree l of the root.
- The remaining nodes will be in the right subtree r.

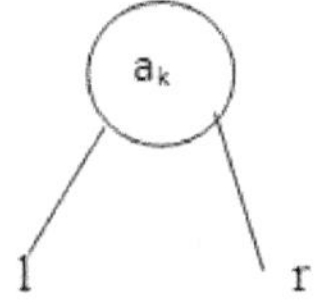

optimal binary search free with root $a_K$

- Define cost (l) =$\sum P(i)*level(ai)+ \sum q(i)*(level(Ei)-1$

          $1\le i\le k$         $0\le i\le k$

- Define cost(r) =$\sum P(i)*level(ai) + \sum q(i)*(level(E_i)-1$

          $k\le i\le n$         $k<i\le n$

- If the tree is optimal then P (k) + cost (l) + cost (r) + w (0, k-1) + w (k, n) must be minimum.

- Cost (l) must be minimum over all binary search tree containing a1, a2 ... $a_{k-1}$ and $E_0$, $E_1$... $E_{k-1}$.

- Similarly cost (r) must be minimum.

- If we use c (i, j) to represent the cost of an optimal binary search tree $t_{ij}$ containing $a_{i+1}$...aj and $E_i$.... $E_j$.

- Tree to be optimal

Cost (l) = cost (0, k-1)  
Cost(r) =c (k,n)

- Substituted cost (l), cost (r) in the following formula.

  P (k) + cost (l) + cost (r) + w (0, k—1) + w (k, n)

  P(k)+c(0,k-l)+c(k,n)+w(0,k-1)+w(k,n)

  Chosen k is minimum

- c (0, n) can be obtained using following formula.

  c(0,n)=min {c(0,k-1)+c(k,n)+P(k)+w(0,k-1)+w(k,n)}

        $1\le k\le n$

- For any c (i, j) we can use the following formula.

  c (i, j) =min {c (i, k-1) + c (k,j) + P (k) + w (i, k-1) + w (k,j)}

        $i\le k\le j$

  c(i,j)= min {c(i,k-1)+c(k,j)} +w(i,j)

        $i\le k\le j$

- The above equation can be solved by first computing all c (i, j) such that j-i= 1.

- Next we can compute all c ( i,j) such that j- i = 2. then all c (i. j) with j - i =3 and so on.
- We record the root r (i,j) of each tree $t_{ij}$, r(i,j) is the value of k that minimizes the equation.

$$c(\,i,j) = \min_{i<k\leq j} \{ c(i, k-1) + c(k,j)\} + w(i,j)$$

### *Example for Optimal Binary Search Tree*

Let n=4 and (a1, a2, a3, a4) = (do if, int, while) let p (1:4) = (3, 3, 1, 1) and q (0:4) = (2, 3, 1, 1, 1). The p's and q's have been multiplied by 16 for convenience. Initially, we have w (i, i) = q (i), c (i, i) = 0 and r (i, 1) = 0, 0≤i≤4.

Find optimal binary search tree.

1.  Initially c (i, i) = 0,

    w(i,i)=q(i)

    r ( i. i) =0

    For all 0≤i≤4.

    i=0   c (0, 0) =0

        w (0,0)=2

        r ( 0, 0) =0

    i=1  c (1, 1) =0

        w (1, 1)=3

        r (1, 1)=0

    i=2   c (2, 2) =0

        w (2,2)= 1

        r (2,2)=0

    i=3  c (3, 3) =0

        w (3,3)= 1

        r (3,3)=0

    i=4  c (4, 4) =0

    w (4,4)=1

    r (4,4)=0

2. First computing all c ( i,j) such that j - i = 1

**i=0, j=1**

w (i,j) = p(j)+q(j)+w(i,j-1)

w (0,1) = 3+3+2=8

c(0,1) =min{c(0,0)+c(1,1)}+w(0,1)

$\qquad$ = min {0+0} +8

$\qquad$ = 8

r (0,1) =1

**i=1, j = 2**

w(1,2)= p(2)+q(2)+w(1,1)

$\qquad$ = 3+1+3

$\qquad$ = 7

c(1,2) =min{c(1, 1)+c(2,2)}+w(1,2)

$\qquad$ =min {0+0} +7

$\qquad$ = 0+7=7

r (1,2) =2

**i = 2, j= 3**

w (2,3) = p(3)+q(3)+w(2,2)

$\qquad$ = 1+1+1

$\qquad$ =3

c(2,3) = min{c(2,2)+c(3,3)}+w(2,3)

$\qquad$ =min (0+0) +w (2, 3)

r (2,3) =3

**i =3, j =4**

w (3,4) = p(4)+q(4)+w(3,3)

$\qquad$ = 1+1+1 =3

c(3,4) = min{c(3,3)+c(4,4) }+w(3,4)

$$=\min\{0+0\}+3$$

$$=3$$

$$r(3,4) = 4$$

3. Compute all c (i, j) such that j- i = 2

**i=0, j=0**

w(0,,2)= p(2)+q(2)+w(0,1)

$$= 3+1+8$$

$$=12$$

c(0,2)= min{c(0,0)+c(1,2)),(c(0, 1)+c(2,2))}+w(0,2)

(k=1 & k=2)

$$= \min \{ (0 + 7), (8 + 0)\} + 12$$

$$= 7+12 = 19$$

When **k =1** we get minimum value c (0, 2) equation.

So   r (0, 2) =**1**

**i=1, j = 3**

w(1,3)= p(3)+q(3)+w( 1,2)

$$= 1+1+7$$

$$= 9$$

c(1,3) = min {c(1, 1)+c(2,3)} +w(1,3)

$$= \min \{0+3\} +9$$

$$= \min \{3\} +9$$

$$=12$$

c (1,3) = min{c (1, 2) +c (3, 3)} +w (1, 3)    k=3

$$= \min \{7+0\} +9 =16$$

k =2 minimizes the c (1,3) equation.

c(1,3) = 12

R (1, 3) = 2

**i=2, j = 4**

w (2,4)= p(4)+q(4)+w(2,3)

$\qquad$ = 1+1+3

$\qquad$ = **5**

c(2,4) =min{c(2,2)+c(3,4)}+w(2,4)

when k=3,

min {0+3}+5=**8**

c (2,4) = min {c(2,3)+c(4.4)} +w(2,4)

When k =4,

min {3 +0} +5 =**8**

Both (k = 3, k = 4) produce some value for c (2, 4).

c (2,4)=**8**

r (2,4)=**3**

4. Computing all (i,j) such that j-1 = 3

$\qquad$ i=0, j=3

$\qquad$ w(0,3)  =p(3)+q(3)+w(0,2)

$\qquad\qquad$ =1+1+12

$\qquad\qquad$ = 14

$\qquad$ c (0,3)  = min { c (0,0) + c (1,3) } + w (0,3)

$\qquad$ k1 $\qquad$ = min {0+12} +14

$\qquad\qquad$ = 26

$\qquad$ c(0,3)  = min {c(0,1)+c(2,3) } +w(0,3)

$\qquad$ k=2 $\qquad$ = min {8+3} +14

$\qquad\qquad$ = 25

$\qquad$ c(0,3)  = min {c(0,2)+c(3,3) } +w(0,3)

$\qquad$ k=3 $\qquad$ =min{19+0}+14

$\qquad\qquad$ =33

When k =2, only minimizes the c (0, 3) equation

c (0,3) = 25

r(0,3) =2

**i=1,j=4**

w (1, 4)  =p(4)+q(4)+w(1,3)

     = 1+1+9

     =11

c(1,4)　=min{c(1,1)+c(2,4)}+w(1,4)

k=2　　=min {0+8} +11

     = 8+11

     =19

c(1,4)　= min { c(1,2)+c(3,4) } +w(1,4)

k=3　　= min{7+3}+11

     =10+11

     =21

c(1,4)　=min { c(1,3)+c(4,4) ) +w(1,4)

k=4　　=min {12+0) +11

     = 12±11

     =23

When k = 2 only minimizes the c (1, 4) equation.

c (1,4) = 19

r (1,4) =2

5. Computing all (i, j) such that j- i= 4

**i=0, j=4**

w (0, 4)= p(4)+q(4)+w(0,3)

     =1 + 1 + 14

     **=16**

c (0,4)  = min {c (0,0) + c (1, 4)) + w (0, 4)}

k=1      = min {0+19} +16

**= 35**

c(0,4)   = min {c(0, 1)+c(2,4)} +w(0,4)

k=2      = min {8+8} +16

= 16+16

=32

c (0, 4) = min {c(0,2)+c(3,4)} +w(0,4)

k=3      =min {19+3} +16

=22+ 16 = 38

c(0,4)   = min{c(0,3)+c(4,4)}+w(0,4)

k=4      = min {25+0} + 16

= 41

6.  All these values specified in the table:

Table 4.1: Computation of C (i,j), w(i,j) r (i,j)

| W00=2 | W11=3 | W22=1 | W33=1 | W44=1 |
|-------|-------|-------|-------|-------|
| C00=0 | C11=0 | C22=0 | C33=0 | C44=0 |
| R00=0 | R11=0 | R22=0 | R33=0 | R44=0 |
| W01=8 | W12=7 | W23=3 | W34=3 | |
| C01=8 | C12=7 | C23=3 | C34=3 | |
| R01=1 | R12=7 | R23=3 | R34=4 | |
| W02=12 | W13=9 | W24=5 | | |
| C01=19 | C13=12 | C24=8 | | |
| R01=1 | R13=2 | R24=3 | | |
| W03=14 | W14=11 | | | |
| C03=25 | C14=19 | | | |
| R03=2 | R14=2 | | | |
| W04=16 | | | | |
| C04=32 | | | | |
| R04=2 | | | | |

c (0, 4) = 32 in the minimum cost of binary search tree for (a1, a,, a3, a4).

7.    The root of tree t04=2=a2

Hence left subtree of a2 = t01 has root a1

Subtree of a1 =t00 &t11

Hence right subtree of a2= t24 = a3

Subtree of a3 = t22 & t34.

8.Construction of t04  i.e optimal binary search tree.

## *Algorithm for Optimal Binary Search Tree Using Dynamic Programming*

```
void OBST (float p [], float q [],int n)
//Given n distinct identifiers a1< a2 <a3 ... an
// p[i], probabilities 1≤i≤n and q[i] .0≤i≤n.
//It computes cost (i, j) of optimal binary search tree tij  for identifier  ai, ai+1 .
//It also computes r {i, j root of tij}
//w (i,j) is the weight of tij.
{
 for(i=0);i<=n—1;i++)
{ //Initialize
w[i, 1]=q[i];
r[i,j] =0;
c[i,1] =0;
//Optimal tree with one node
w [i, i+I] = q [i] + q [i+1] + p [i+1];
r [i, i+l,j ]= i+l;
c [I, i+1] q [i] + q [i+l] + p [i+l];
}
w(n,n)=q[n];
r [n, n] =0;
 c[n,n]=0;
```

```cpp
// Find optimal trees with m nodes

for (m=2; m< = n; m++)

 for (i =0; 1 < n-m; i++)

j=i+m;

w[i,j]=w[i,j-1]+P[j]+q[j];

k =find (C, r, i,j);

//A value of 1 in the range r [i,j-1} ≤l

//l≤r [i+1,j] that minimizes c [i, l -1]+ c [l,j]

c [i,j] = w [i,j] + c [i, k-i] + c [k,j];

r[i,j]=k;

}

cout <<c [0] [n] <<"";

cout <<w [0] [n]<<" ";

cout<<r [0] [n]<<"" "";

}

int  find (c, r, i, j)

{ min=α;

for (m =r [i] [j- 1] to r[i + I][j]) do

{

if ( c [i] [m-I] + c [m] [j] <min)

{ min=c[i][m-1]+c[m][j];

 l=m

}

return (I);

}

}
```

### *Complexity of Optimal Binary Search Tree*

The complexity of an algorithm depends on space and time.

### *Space Complexity*

Storage space for probabilities of p [ ] n location Successful search

Storage space for probabilities of q [ ] = n location

Unsuccessful search

Storage space for cost array c [ ] [ ] = $n^2$ location

Storage space for weight array w [ ] [ ] = $n^2$ location

Dynamic programming technique

Storage space for root array r [ ] [ ] = $n^2$ location

Storage space for n m= 2 location

Storage space for control variable requires i, j, k = 3 location

Total storage space = [ $2n + 3n^2 + 5$ ]

### *Time Complexity*

The computation of c (i,j) requires = 0 (m) time.

The total time for all c (i,j) requires= 0 (nm -$m^2$)

With j -i = m

The total time to evaluate   $\sum$ (nm - $m^2$)= 0 ($n^3$)

All the c(i,j)'s&r(i,j)

The 'tΦn' can be constructed from the value of r (i, j) = 0 (n)

**Total time complexity = [ 0 ($n^3$) ]**

## 4.4. 0/1 Knapsack Problem Concept

Given n items of known weights w1, w2.... wn and profits P1, P2 and a knapsack capacity m. find the most valuable subset of the item that fit in to the knapsack.

A solution to the knapsack problem can be obtained by making a sequence of decision on the variables x1, x2..... xn. A decision variable x1 involves determining which of the values '0' (or) 'I' is to be assigned to it.

### *Principal of Optimality*

Let us assume that decision on the $x_1$ are made in the order $x_1$, $x_2$,..$x_n$. Following a decision on x, we may in one of 2 possible stages:

1. The capacity remaining in the knapsack is m, no profit has gained.
2. The capacity remaining is m-w and a profit of P has gained.

It is clear that the remaining decisions $x_{n-1}$ .. . .$x_n$ must be optimal with respect to the problem state resulting from the decision on x.

### *Example 1*

Let us consider the instance given by the following data:

| Item | weight | profit |
|------|--------|--------|
| 1 | 2 | 12 |
| 2 | 1 | 10 |
| 3 | 3 | 20 |
| 4 | 2 | 15 |

### *Capacity w = 5 find the Optimal Solution for Knapsack Problem*

1. Define the initial condition

    P[0,j]=0 for j>=0 & p[i,0]=0 for i>=0

    So, P(0,0)=0        P(1,0)=0

    P(0,1)=0   P(2,0)=0

    P(0,2) =0   P(3,0) =0

    P(0,3) =0   P(4,0) =0

    P (0,4) = 0

2. The item i's weight & profit [ W1 = 2, P1 = 12]

    Compute P (i,j) using the formula

    P (i,j)=max {P (i-1,j), Pi +P (i- 1,j-$w_i$)} if j -$w_i$ > = 0

    P(i,j)= P(i-1,j) if j-$w_i$<0

    Compute p(1,2)=Max {P(i- 1,j) ,Pi+ P(i-1, j-$w_i$)}

    Compute P(1,2)=Max { P (0, 2), 12 + P (0,1 )}

    = Max{0,12+0}

$$= 12$$

Compute P (1,3) = max {P (0,3), 12 + 0}

$$= \max\{0,12\}$$

$$= 12$$

Compute P (1,4) = max { P (0,4), 12 + P (0, 3)}

$$= \max(0,12+0)$$

$$= [12]$$

Compute P(1,5) = max {P(0,5), 12+P(0,3)}

$$= \max\{0,12+0\}$$

$$= 12$$

3. The item 2's weight and profit w2=1, p2 = 10

Compute p (2, 1) = max { P (1,1), 10 + P (1, 0)}

$$= \max\{0,10+0\}$$

$$= 10$$

Compute p (2,2)  = max {P (1,2), 10 + 0(1, 1)}

$$= \max\{12,10+0)$$

$$= \max \{12, 10)$$

$$= 12$$

Compute P(2,3)  = max{P(1,3),10+P(1,2)}

$$= \max\{12,10+12\}$$

$$= 22$$

Compute p (2, 4) = max { p (1,4), 10+ P (1,3)}

$$= \max\{12,10+12\}$$

$$= 22$$

Compute p (2, 5) = max (P (1,5), 10 + P (1,4))

$$= \max\{12,10+12\}$$

$$= 22$$

4. The item 3's weight and profit W3=3, P3 =20

    Compute P (3,1)  = max{P(2,1)}

                  =10

    Compute P (3,2)  = max{P(2,2)}

                  = 12

    Compute P (3,3)  = max {P (2,3), 20+ P (2,0)) max(22,20+0}

                  = 22

    Compute P (3,4)  =max { P (2,4), 20+ P (2,1)) max{22,20+ 10)

                  = 30

    Compute P (3,5)  = max {P(2,5),20+P(2,2)) max{22,20+12}

                  = 32

5. The item 4's weight and profit W4 = 2, P4 = 15

    Compute P(4, 1) =max{P(3,1)}

                  = 10

    Compute P (4, 2) = max {P(3,2), 15+P(3,0)}

                  = max(12,15+0)

                  = 15

    Compute P (4, 3) =max { P(3,3), 15+P(3,1)}

                  = max(22,15+10)

                  = 25

    Compute P(4, 4) = max { P (3,4), 15 + P (3,2) }

                  =max {30, 15+ 12}

                  =30

    Compute P(4,5)  = max {P (3, 5), 15 ÷ P (3, 3))

                  = max {32,15+22}

                  =37

|  | j | 0 | 1 | 2 | 3 | 4 | 5 |
|---|---|---|---|---|---|---|---|
|  | i |  |  |  |  |  |  |
|  | 0 | 0 | 0 | 0 | 0 | 0 | 0 |
| W1=2, P1=12 | 1 | 0 | 10 | 12 | 12 | 12 | 12 |
| W2=1, P2=10 | 2 | 0 | 10 | 12 | 22 | 22 | 22 |
| W3=3, P3=20 | 3 | 0 | 10 | 12 | 22 | 30 | 32 |
| W4=2 P4=15 | 4 | 0 | 10 | 15 | 25 | 30 | 37 |

Thus the maximum value is P [4, 5]= 37

We can find the composition of an optimal subset by tracing back the computation of the entry in the table.

- p[4,5]!= p[3, 5] so item 4 included in the solution set
- Knapsack capacity= 5, weight of an item 4 is 2, 5 - 2= 3 remaining units of the knapsack capacity.
- P [3, 3] =P [2, 3] so item3 is not included
- P [2,3]!= P [1, 3] so item 2 is included in the solution set
- The remaining capacity of knapsack is 3, weight of item 2 is I i.e., 3 - I = 2.
- p[1,2]!=p[0,2] item 1 is included in the solution set.

**Optimal solution {(1, 2, 4)}**

## *Algorithm for 0/1 Knapsack Problem*

```
void D knap (P, w, x , n, m)

{

K[0]=1

Pair[1].p=pair[1];w=0.0;

M=1, n=1;

b [I] next = 2 //next free spot in pair []

for (1=1; i< n; i++)

{

// generate S'

k =t;
```

```
u =Largest (pair,w, t, h, i, m)

for (int j= t;j <u;j ++)

// generate S1' and merge

pp=Pair[j] .p+p[i];

ww=pair[j].w+w[i];

// (pp,ww) is the next element in Si-1;

While ((k < h) and (pair [k]. w≤ ww))

{

Pair [next]. p = Pair [k]. p;

Pair [next]. w = pair [k] . w;

Next= next + 1;

k=k+ 1;

}

if((k <= h) & (pair [k]. w = ww))

{

if (pp <pair [k]. p)

pp = pair [k]. p;

k=k+1

}

if(pp> pair [next - 1] .p)

{

Pair [next] .p =pp;

 Pair [next] .w =ww;

Next= next + 1;

}

While (( k <= h & (pair [k]. p <= pair [next -1] .p))

k=k+1; }
```

// merging remaining terms from S'-1

While (k < = h)

Pair [next]. P= pair [k]. P;

 Pair [next] .w = pair [k]. w;

 Next=next+ 1;

 k=k+ 1;

Inilialize for' S'

T=h+l;

h =next -1;

 b[i+ l]=next;

Traceback (P, w, pair, x, m, n);

### *Complexity of 0/1 Knapsack Problem*

Time complexity

Time needed to compute all the S1's = 0 (2^n)

Time needed for traceback = 0 (n^2)

Total time for 0/1 knapsack problem =0 (2^n)

## 4.5. The Travelling Sales man Problem

### *Concept*

Let G =(V,E) be a directed graph with edge costs Cij. The variable Cij defined such that Cij>0 for all i and j and Cij=α if(i,j) ε E . Let IVI=n and n>i.

A tour of G is a directed. Simple cycle that includes every vertex in V. The cost tour is the sum of the cost of the edges on the tour. The travelling salesperson Problem is to find a tour of minimum cost.

### *Procedure to Find Sales Person Problem*

A tour to be a simple path that starts and ends at vertex 1.

Every tour consists of an edge (1, k) for some k € V - { 1} and a path from vertex k to vertex 1.

The path from vertex k to vertex 1 goes through each vertex in V -{ 1, k } exactly once.

- If the tour is optimal then the path from k to 1 must be a shortest. k to 1 going through all vertices in V - {1, k}
- Let g (i ,S) be the length of a shortest path starting at vertex i. going through all verities in S and terminating all vertex 1.
- The function g (1, v- {1}) is the length of an optimal sales person tour

  g (1, V- {1})=min{c1k + g (k, V- {1, k})} 2≤k≤n
- Generalizing the above equation g (i, S) = min{cij ,g{j, S -{j}}
- g(i,Φ)=Ci1        1≤i≤n
- To obtain g (i, S) for all S of size i
- Then we can obtain g (1, S) for |S|= 2 and so on

### *Example for Travelling Sales Person Problem*

Consider the following directed graph. The edge lengths are given by matrix C. Find the minimum tour cost.

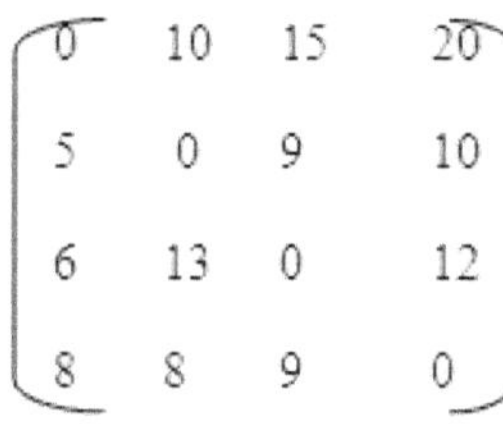

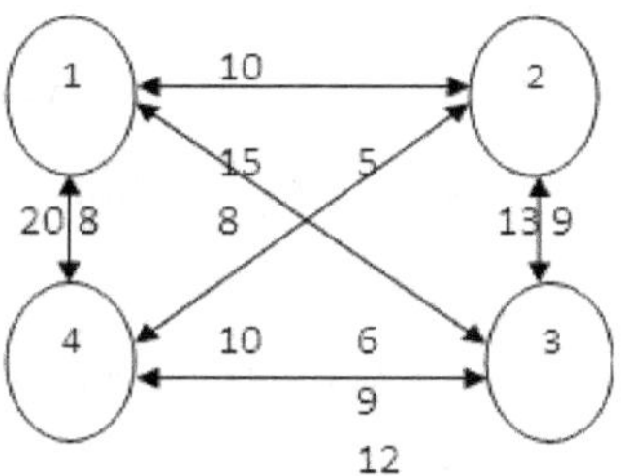


1.  compute  g(2,Φ)=c21=5

    g(3,Φ)=c31=6

    g(4,Φ)=c41=8

1.  We compute g (i, S) with |S| = I

    g(2,{3})= C23+g(3, Φ)

        = 9+6= 15

    g(2,{4)) = C24+g(4, Φ)

        = 10+8

        =18

$g(3,\{2\}) = C32 + g(2, \Phi)$

$\qquad = 13 + 5$

$\qquad = 18$

$g(3,\{4\}) = C34 + g(4,)$

$\qquad = 12 + 8$

$\qquad = 20$

$g(4.\{2\}) = C42 + g(4,4)$

$\qquad = 8 + 5$

$\qquad = 13$

$g(4, \{3\}) = C43 + g(3, 0)$

$\qquad = 9 + 6$

$\qquad = 15$

Next we compute g (i, S) with |S| = 2

$g(2,\{3,4\}) \quad = \min \{ C23 + g(3, \{4\}), C24 + g(4\{3\}) \}$

$\qquad = \min \{ (9+20), (10-15) \}$

$\qquad = 25$

$g(3, \{2,4\}) \quad = \min (C32 + g(2, \{4\}), C34 + g(4, (2)) \}$

$\qquad = \min \{ (13+18), (12+ 13) )$

$\qquad = 25$

$g (4, \{2, 3\}) \ = \min \{C42 + g (2, \{3\}), C43 (3, \{2\}) \}$

$\qquad = \min\{8+15), (9+18)\}$

$\qquad = 23$

Finally compute g (i, S) with |S| = 3

$g (1, (2,3,4)) \ = \min (C12 + g(2, \{3, 4\}), C13 + g(3, \{2,4\}), C14 + g(4, (2,3)))$

$\qquad = \min ((10 + 25), (15 + 25), (20 + 23))$

$\qquad = \min\{35,40,43)$

$\qquad = 35$

*Optimal tour of the Graph has Length 35.*

A tour length can be constructed if we retain with g (i, S) the value of j that minimizes.

g(i,S)=min{cij+g(j,S-{j})}

So J (1, (2,3,4) ) = 2. Thus the tour starts from 1and goes to 2

The remaining tour can be obtained from g (2, (3,4) ). So J (2, {3,4}) = 4

The next edge is (2,4). The remaining tour is g (4, {3})

So, J(4,{3})=3

The optimal tour is 1, 2, 4, 3, 1

Minimum cost length =35

*Complexity of Traveling Sales Person Problem*

Computation of g(i, S) with I S I= k requires k comparison

It will require O((n^2 )(2^n)) time

**1. How will you construct an optimal binary search tree? (May /June '06)**

A binary search tree is one of the most important data structures in computer science. Its principal application is to implement a dictionary. a set of elements with the operations of searching, insertion and deletion. If probabilities of searching for elements of a set are known as optimal binary search tree, it requires only average number of comparison.

**2. What is dynamic programming?**

Dynamic programming is an algorithm design technique for solving problem with overlapping sub programs. The smaller sub programs are solved only once and recording the results in a table from which the solution to the original problem is obtained.

**3. What is meant by all pair shortest path problem?**

Given a weighted connected graph, the all pair shortest path problem is to find the distance from each vertex to all other vertices.

**4. Define war shall's algorithm.**

Warshall's algorithm is an application of dynamic programming technique which  is used to find  the transitive closure of a directed graph.

**5. Define floyd's algorithm.**

Floyd's algorithm is an application of dynamic programming, which is used to find the all pairs shortest path problem.

It is applicable to both directed and undirected weighted graph, but they do not contain a cycle of negative length.

**6. Define principle of optimality? Or define optimality.**

The principle of optimality says that an optimal solution to any instance of a problem is composed of optimal solution to its sub instances.

**7. What is the general procedure for dynamic programming?**

- It is an algorithm design method that can be used when solution to a problem can viewed as the result of sequence of decisions.
- Enumerate all decision sequences and then pick out the best.
- Optimal sequence of decision is obtained.

### 8. What are the usage of multistage graph?

The multistage graph is to find a minimum cost path from source 's' to sink 't' i.e. destination. The cost of a path from 's' to 't' is the sum of the cost of the edges on the path.

### 9. What is complexity of multistage graph?

### Time Complexity

Finding the minimum cost for each and every edge $= 0(V + |E|)$

Shortest path from source 'S' to sink 't' in k stages $= 0(k)$

### Space Complexity

Storage space for cost array cost [] = n location

Storage space for minimum cost path array P [] = n location

Storage space for decision array d [] = n location

Storage space for stage 'k' variable = 1

Storage space for variable 'n' = 1

Storage variable 'j' = 1

Total storage space $3n + 3 = 3 (n + I)$

### 10. What are the application of multistage graph problem

Application of multistage problem

### Resource Allocation Problem

- n units of resource are to be allocated to 'r' projects
- The problem is to allocate the resource to r projects in such a way to maximize total net profit

### 11. What is the formula used in floyed's algorithm.

### Shortest Path

$Ak(i,j) = min\{A(k—1)(i,j), A(k—1l(i,k) + A(k-1)(k,j)\}$

$A°(i,j) = w(i,j)$

Where w = weight matrix

K = intermediate vertex

### 12. What is the time complexity of all pair shortest path problem?

**Time Complexity**

For finding all pair shortest path algorithm uses 3 loops.

So time complexity is 0(n3).

### 13. What is the formula used for cost of binary search tree?

Cost of binary search tree = cost of successful search + cost of unsuccessful

$$= \sum p(i) * \text{level (ai) (for } 1<=i<=n) + q(i) * (\text{level (Ei-1) (for } 0<=i<=n)$$

P (i) = Probability of successful search for node i

level (ai) = Level for node i

q (i) = Probability of unsuccessful search for node i

### 14. How to find the root in binary search tree.

The root r (i, j) of binary search tree tij, is the value of k that minimizes the  Cost function.

$$C (i, i) = \min \{( C (i, k - 1) + c (k, j) \} + w (i, j)$$

### 15. What is the time complexity of optimal binary search tree.

The computation of c(i, j) requires =0 (m) time

The total time for all c(i, j)'s with (j - i= m) = 0 (nm -m^2)

The total time to evaluate$\sum$ (nm -m^2) =0 (n3)

The 'tΦn' can be constructed from the values of r (i, j) = 0(n)

Total time complexity= 0 (n3)

### 16. What is meant by 0/1 knapsack problem

Given n items of known weights w1, w2.... wn and profits P1, P2 and a knapsack capacity m. find the most valuable subset of the item that fit in to the knapsack.

A solution to the knapsack problem can be obtained by making a sequence of decision on the variables x1, x2..... xn. A decision variable x1 involves determining which of the values '0' (or) 'I' is to be assigned to it.

### 17. What is the time complexity of knapsack problem.

Time needed to compute all the S1's = 0 (2^n)

Time needed for traceback = 0 (n^2)

Total time for 0/1 knapsack problem =0 (2^n)

### 18. Define travelling sales person problem?

Let G (V. E) be directed graph with edge cost Cij. The variable cij defined such that cij>0   for all  i and j , cij=$\alpha$ .Let IVI=n and n>1.

A tour of G is a directed simple cycle that includes every vertex in V. The cost of a tour is the sum of the cost of the edges on the tour.

The travelling sales person problem is to find a tour of minimum cost.

### 19. What is the time complexity of traveling sales person problem.

The computation of g (i, S) with S = k requires k -1 comparison

Total time = 0 (n^2 x 2^n)

### 20. What is the application of traveling sales person problem.

***Application of Sales Person Problem***

### 1.  Postal Van

- The route taken by the postal van is a tour
- One vertex represents the post office from which the postal van starts and to which it must return.

### 2.  Use a robot arm to tighten the nuts on some piece of machinery on an assembly line

- The robot arm will start from its initial position successively move to each of the remaining nuts and return to the initial position.
- The path of the arm is clearly a tour on a graph in which vertices represent the nuts.

### 3.  Production Environment

- In a production environment, several commodities are manufactured on the same set of machines.

# Unit 5

## Backtracking

Backtracking: General Method – 8 Queens problem – sum of subsets – graph coloring – Hamiltonian problem – Knapsack problem - Branch and Bound – Assignment Problem

### 5.1. Backtracking

The basic idea is to construct solutions for one component at a time and evaluate as follows.

If the sequence of choices represented by a current node of the state space tree can be developed further without violating the problems constraint, it is done by considering the first remaining legitimate option for the next component. Otherwise if there is no legitimate options for the next component, the algorithms backtrack to replace the last component of the partially constructed solution with its next option.

It is a kind of solving a problem by trial and error. We make sure that we never thing twice, we also make sure that if the problem is finite, we will eventually try all possibilities.

Backtracking problems require that all the solutions satisfy a complex set of constraints.

Two types of constraints are:

1. Implicit constraint
2. Explicit constraint.

#### 1. *Implicit Constraint*

The implicit constraints are rules that determine which of the tuples in the Solution space of 1 satisfy the criterion function.

The implicit constraint describe the way in which the $x_i$ must relate to each other.

#### 2. *Explicit Constraint*

Explicit constraints are rule that restrict each x to take on values from a given set.

Example

$x_i > 0$ or $S_i$ {All non negative real numbers}

$x_i = 0$ or $x_i = 1$, $S_i$ {0, 1}

### Criterion Function

The desired solution is expressible as an n tuples $(x_1, x_2 \ldots x_n)$, where the $x_i$ are chosen from finite set $S_i$.

The problem to be solved calls for finding one vector that maximizes a criterion function $P(x_1, x_2 \ldots x_n)$.

### Examples for Backtracking

### Example 1: 8 Queen Problem

To place 8 queens on an 8 x 8 chess bound so that no 2 "attack" i.e., no. them are on the same rows and columns and diagonals of the chess board.

### Criterion Function

All solution to the 8 queens problem can be represented as 8 tuples$(x_1, x_2 \ldots x_8)$ where $x_i$ is the column on which queen 'i' is placed.

### Explicit Constraints

Explicit constraint $S_{i=} \{1, 2, 3, 4, 5, 6, 7, 8)$ $1 \leq i \leq 8$ .The solution space consists of $8^8$ tuples.

### Implicit Constraints

The implicit constraints for this problem are that no 2 $x_i$'s can be the column or diagonal.

### Solution Set

The solution set contains the following value.

S={4,6,8,2,7, 1,3,5}

| 1 | 2 | 3 | 4 | 5 | 6 | 7 | 8 |
|---|---|---|---|---|---|---|---|
|   |   |   | Q1 |   |   |   |   |
|   |   |   |   |   | Q2 |   |   |
|   |   |   |   |   |   |   | Q3 |
|   | Q4 |   |   |   |   |   |   |
|   |   |   |   |   |   | Q5 |   |
| Q6 |   |   |   |   |   |   |   |
|   |   | Q7 |   |   |   |   |   |
|   |   |   |   | Q8 |   |   |   |

Solution to 8 Queen's Problem

### Example 2: Sum of Subset Problem

Given positive numbers $w_i$, $1 \leq i \leq n$ and m the problem calls for finding all subsets of the $w_i$, whole sum are m.

The solution can be represented in 2 ways.

### 1. Solution Set Represented in Method I

### Criterion Function

All solutions are k tuples $(x_1, x_2 \ldots .x_k)$ $1 \leq k \leq n$ and different solutions may have different sized tuples.

### Explicit Constraint

The explicit constraint require $x_i \in \{j/j$ is an integer and $1 \leq j \leq n\}$

### Implicit Constraint

The implicit constraint require that no 2 $x_i$ be the some and that sum of the corresponding $w_i$'s be m.

### Ex: n=4 , (w1, w2, w3, w4) = (11,13,24, T) and m=31.

### Solution Set

Solution set Si = {(11, 13. 7). (24. 7)}

Solution described by the vector, (1, 2, 4) & (3, 4)

### 2. Solution set Represented in Method II

### Criterion Function

Each solution subset is represented by an n tuple.

$\{x_1, x_2, \ldots ., x_n\}$

$x_i \in \{0,1\}$ $1 \leq I \leq n$

if $x_i=0$, the $w_i$, not chosen

if $x_i=1$, the $w_i$ is chosen.

All solution using fixed size tuples.

## *Explicit Constraint*

The explicit constraint require $x_i \in \{ j / j$ is an integer and $l \le j \le n \}$

## *Implicit Constraint*

It require that no $2x_i$ be the same and that the sum corresponding $w_i$'s be m.

## *Example: n =4, (w1, w2, w3, w4) = (11, 13, 24, 7) and m = 31.*

## *Solution Set*

Solution set $S_i = \{(1, 1,0, 1), (0,0\ 1, 1)\}$

## *General Method*

- Backtracking algorithm determine problem solutions by systematically searching the solution space for the given problem instance.
- It is performed by using tree organization for the solution space.
- A state space tree for a backtracking algorithm is constructed using depth search.
- The root of the space tree represents an initial state before the search for a solution begins.
- The node of the first level in the tree represents the choice made for the first component of a solution.
- The nodes of the second level represent the choices for the $2^{nd}$, component and so on.
- A node in a state space tree is said to be promising if it correspond to a partially constructed solution that may still lead to a complete solution.
- If the current node is non promising, then the algorithm backtracks to the node's parent to consider the next possible option for its last component.
- A node which has been generated and all of whose children have not yet been generated is called a live node.
- The live node whose children are currently being generated is called the E-node (node being expanded)
- A dead node is a generated node which is not to be expanded further or all of whose children have been generated.
- Finally if the algorithm reaches a complete solution to the problem, then it either stops or backtracks to continue searching for other possible solution.

## *Examples for State Space Tree Organization*

### *Example 1: 4 Queens Problem*

- 4 queens are to be placed on 4 x 4 chess board, so that no 2 attack ie no 2 queens are on the same row, column or diagonal.
- We start with the empty board and then place queen 1 in the first possible position ie (1, 1) row 1, column 1.
- Queen 2 cannot be placed in (2, 1) & (2, 2) so acceptable position is (2, 3) ie row2, column 3.
- This position proves to be dead end, because there is no acceptable position for queen 3. So the algorithm backtracks and puts queen 2 in the next possible position at (2, 4) ie row 2, column 4.
- The queen 3 is placed at (3, 2) ie row 3, column 2, this lead dead end.
- The algorithm backtracks queen 1 and moves it to (1, 2) ie row 1, colunm 2.
- Queen 2 cannot be placed in (2, 1), (2, 2), (2, 3) so acceptable position is row 2, column 4.
- Queen 3 is placed at (3. 1) ie row 3, column 1.
- Queen 4 cannot be placed in (4, 1), (4, 2). So acceptable position is (4, 3).

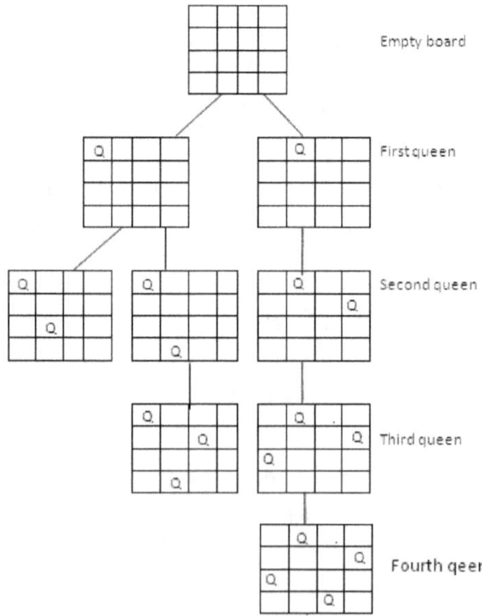

- Solution space consists of all 4! permutations of the 4 tuple (1, 2, 3.4)

- The left most sub tree contains all solutions with $x_1=1$

- The next sub tree contains all solutions with $x_2 = 2$

- The right most sub tree contains all solutions with $x_1=4$

- The solution space is defined by all paths from the root node to a leaf node. There are 4!= 24 leaf nodes in the tree.

The possible solution is

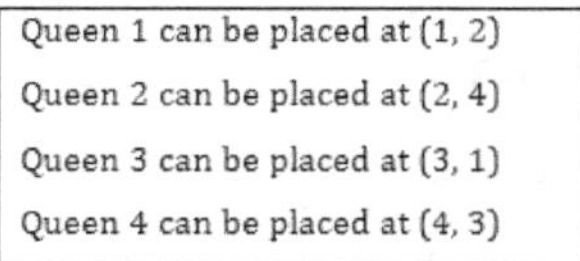


## *Example 2: Sum of Subsets*

- At each node, the solution space is partitioned into sub solution.

- The solution space is defined by all paths from the root node to any node in the tree, since any such path corresponds to a subset satisfying the explicit constraints.

- The left-most sub tree of the root defines all sub sets containing $w_1$, the next sub tree defines all subset containing $w_2$ and so on.

- If n=4, $(w_1, w_2, w_3, w_4)$ = (11, 13, 24, 7) and m=31.

- The possible paths are (1), (1, 2), (1,2, 3), (1,2, 3,4), (1,2, 4),(1, 3.. (2, 3) and so on.

- Thus the left sub tree of the root contains all sub sets containing $w_1$; the right sub tree defines all subsets not containing $w_1$ and so on.

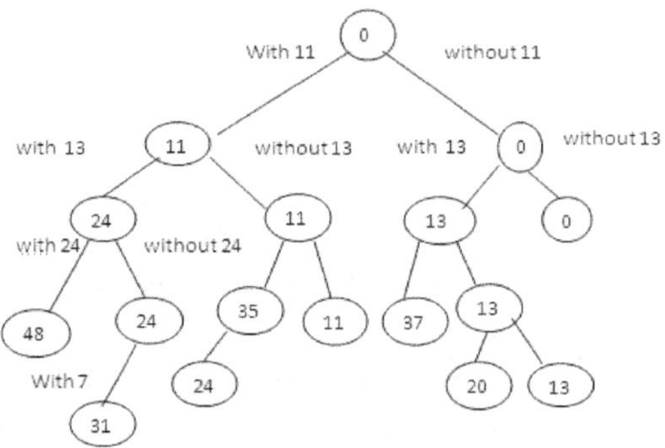


Fig. 5.1: Solution Space Organization for the Sum of Subsets Nodes are Numbered in Breadth First Search

## *Method 2*

- Leaf nodes are solution states.
- Answer states are those solution states 's' for which the path from the root to s defines a tuple that is a member of the set of solution of the problem.
- At level 1 the tree partitioning could corresponds to $x_1 = 0$ and $x_1 = 1$.
- At level 2, the partitioning could correspond to $x_2 = 0$ and $x_2 = 1$.
- At level 3 it could correspond to $x_3 = 0$ and $x_3 = 1$ and so on.

## *Recursive Backtracking Algorithm*

Void Backtrack (k)

//This schema describes the backtracking process

// Using recursion

//x [1], x [2], . . . .x [k-1] of the solution vector

{

for (each x [k]  T (x [1], x[2],.....x [k-1]) do

{

if (BK (x [1], x[2] x[k]≠ 0) then

{ if(x[l],x[2],.. x[k]is a path to an answer node

Output (x [1: k]);

If (k <n) then Backtrack (k+ 1);

}

}

}

- Let (c) be a path a from the root to a node in a state space tree.
- T $(x_1, x_2 . . . .x_i)$ be the set of all possible values for $x_{i+1}$ such that $(x_1, x_2 . . . .x_{i+1})$ is path to problem state.
- The solution vector $(x_1, x_2 . . . .x_n)$ is treated as global array x [1] [n]
- If $B_{i+1}$ $(x_1, x_2 . . . .x_{i+1})$ is false for a path $(x_1, x_2 . . . .x_{i+1})$ from the root node to a problem state, then the path cannot be extended to reach an answer node.

### *General Iterative Backtracking Method*

```
void IBacktrack (n)

//This schema describes the backtracking process.

//All solutions are generated in x [1: n] and printed.

{

k= 1;

While (k≠0)

{

if (there remains an untried x [k] ∈

T(x[1],x[2]..... x [k-1]) and

 Bk(x[1],x[2] ........x[k]) is true

{

    if(x [1], ...... x[k] is a path to an Answer node)

    Output(x[l : k];

    k=k+1;

    //consider the next set

}

else

k=k-1;//Backtrack to previous set.

}

}
```

- The T ( ) will yield the set of possible values that can be placed as the first component $x_i$ of the solution vector.
- The component $x_1$ will take on those values for which the bounding $B_i (x_i)$ is true.
- The variable k is continually incremented and a solution vector is grown until either a solution is found or no untried value of $x_k$ remains.
- When k is decremented, the algorithm must resume the generation of possible elements for the $k^{th}$ position that have not yet been tried.

### *Time Complexity*

There are 4 factors that determine the time required by a backtracking algorithm

The time to generate the next $x_k$ i.e., solution node

The number of $x_k$(solution node) satisfying the explicit constraints

Time for the bounding functions $B_k$.

The number of solution nodes generated.

Number of nodes in the solution space=n!

Worst case time complexity=$O(p(n))n!$

## 5.2. Eight Queens Problem

### *Concept*

The problem is to place n queens on an n by n chessboard, so that no 2 queens attack each other being in the same row (or) in the same column or in the same column or in the same diagonal. A chess board has 8 x 8 fields.

It is possible to place 8 queens on this board, so that no 2 queens can attack each other.

### *5.2.1. Solution for 8 Queens Problem*

Placing Queen on chessboard, we have to check 3 conditions.

- No 2 Queens on the same row
- No 2 Queens on the same column
- No 2 Queens on the same diagonal.

To identify whether the 2 Queens on the some diagonal.

It must satisfy following conditions.

- Every element on the same diagonal that runs from the upper left to the lower right have same (row-column) value ie (4, 2), (5, 3), (3, 1) (6, 4) (7, 5),(8,6) all these have some row- column value =2.

- Also every element on the same diagonal that goes from the upper right to the lower left have the same (row+column) value ie (1, 8), (2, 7) (3, 6), (4, 5) (5, 4) (6, 3) (7, 2), (8. 1).

All these square have same (row + column) value ie row + column = 9.

## Example

Suppose 2 queens are placed at positions (i, j) and (k, *l*)

To identify whether they are placed on the same diagonal

$$|j\text{-}l| = |i\text{-}k|$$

## Procedure

- We start with the empty board and then place queen 1 in the first possible position ie (1, 1) row I, column 1.
- Queen 2 is placed at (2, 8) ie row 2,

  Queen 3 is placed at (3, 6) ie row 3,

  Queen 4 is placed at (4, 3) ie row 4,

  Queen 5 is placed at (5, 7) ie row 5,

  Queen 6 is placed at (6, 2) ie row 6,

  Queen 7 is placed at (7, 4) ie row 7,

  Queen 8 cannot place at 5th position.
- So Backtrack the position of queen 1. Queen 1 is placed at (1, 2) ie row 1 column 2.
- Queen 2 is placed at (2, 4) ie row 2, column 4.

  Queen 3 is placed at (3, 1) ie row 3, column 1.

  Queen 4 is placed at (4, 3) ie row 4, column 3.

  Queen 5 is placed at (5, 5) ie row 5, column 5.

  Queen 6 cannot be placed at (6, 6) (6, 7) &(6,8).so it reaches dead end,backtrack the position of queen 1.
- Queen 1 is placed at (1,3) ierow 1, column 3.

  Queen 2 is placed at (2,6) ie row 2, column 6.

  Queen 3 is placed at (3, 2) ie row 3, column 2.

  Queen 4 is placed at (4,7) ie row 4, column 7.

  Queen 5 is placed at (5,1) ie row 5, column 1.

  Queen 6 is placed at (6,4) ie row 6, column 4.

  Queen 7 is placed at (7,8) ie row 7, column 8.

  Queen 8 is placed at(8,5) ie row 8, column 5.

It is one of the required solutions for 8 Queen's problem.

### 5.2.2. *Algorithm for 8 Queen's Problem*

```
void Place (k, i)
To find 2 Queens in the same col (or) diagonal
//Returns true if a queen can be placed in
//kth row and ith column otherwise it return false.
// x[ ] is a global axing whose first (k-1) values have been set.
// Abs (r) returns the absolute value of r.
{
    for(j- l ; j <k; j++)
    if((x[j]== i)) //in the same col
    or (Abs(x[j]-i)=Abs(j-k)
    //or in the same diagonal
    return(false)
    else
    return (true)
}
// All solution to the n Queens Problem
Voids NQueens (k, n)
// Using backtracking, this procedure prints all
//possible placements of n queens on n x n
//chess board, so that they are non attacking
{
    for (i=1; i<=n; i++)
    {
        if place (k , i)
        {
         x [k] =i;
        if(k= =n)
        cout<<x [i] [n];
        else
        NQueens (k+1, n);
        }
    }
}
```

### *Complexity of 8 Queens Problem*

- In 8 x 8 chess board, there are (64) possible ways to place 8 queens.
- To place queen, on distinct rows and column, we need to examine at most 8!
- or only 40, 320, tuples.
- The total number of nodes in the 8 queens state space tree is 69, 281.
- The estimated number of unbounded nodes is only about 2.34% of the total number of nodes in the 8 queens state space tree.
- Initially we can select any one of n value for queen 8 and so on.
- We can select any one of n-1 values for queen 2 and so on.
- Finally we can select one remaining value for queen 8.
- Therefore it tests 8! configuration is 40320.
- So it requires $t(n) = \text{def } n!$

## 5.3. Sum of Subsets

### *Concept*

We are given n distinct positive numbers (usually called weights) and we desire to find all combination of these numbers, whose sum, are 'm'. This is called sum of subsets problem.

### *5.3.1.  Solution to Sum of Subsets Problem*

- Sort the weights in non decreasing (ascending) order.
- The root of the space tree represents the starting point, with no decision about the given elements.
- Its left and right child represents inclusion and exclusion of $x_i$ in a set.
- The node to be expanded, cheek it with the following condition

$$w_i x_i + w_{i+1} \leq m$$

- The bounded node can be identified with the following condition.

$$Bk(x_1, x_2, \ldots, x_k) = \text{tree}$$
$$\text{if } w_i x_i + w_i \geq m$$

- Backtrack the bounded node and find alternative solution.
- Thus a path from the root to a node on the $i^{th}$ level of the tree indicates which of the first i numbers have been included in the subsets represented by that node.

- We can terminate the node as non promising if either of the 2 inequalities holds

$$S^{\cdot} = w_i x_i$$

S' + $w_{i+1}$ > m (where S' in too large)

S' + $w_{i+1}$ <m (where S' in too small)

### 5.3.2. Example for Sum of Subset Problem

### Example 1

Let w ={5, 10. 12. 13, 15, 18) and, m = 30. Find all possible sub sets of 'w'that sum to 'm' and draw state space tree.

Solution set = {(5, 10,15), (5, 12, 13), (12, 18)} solution set can also represented in another way

Solution set {(1, 1,0,0 1,0), (1,0, 1, 1,0,0), (0,0, 1,0,0, 1)}

### Example 2

Let w={3,5,6,7} & and rn=15.Find all possible subsets of 'w' that sum to'm' and draw thé state space tree.

### 5.3.3. Algorithm for Sum of Subsets Problem

// Recursive backtracking algorithm for sum of subsets problem.

void sum of sub (s, k, r)

//Find all subsets of w [1: n] that sum to m.

//The w[j]'s are in non decreasing order

{

// Generate left child

//s+w[ ki s m since $B_{k-1}$ is true

    X[kJ= 1;

    if(s+w [kJ = = m)

    output (x [1: k]) ; // subset found

// There is no recursive call w [j]> 0.

    else (s+w[k] + w[k+l] ≤m)

    Sum of sub (s+w [k],k+1, r—w [kl)

//v-sum of all weights in a given set.

// Generate right child and evaluate $B_K$.

```
if((s+r -w [k]≥ m) and (s+w [k+1]≤m))

{

s[k]=0

sum of sub(s,k+1,r-w[k]);

}}
```

### 5.3.4. Complexity of Sum of Subsets Problem

- The algorithm splits arbitrarily N elements into 2 sets of N/2 each.
- For each of these 2 sets, it calculates sum of all $2^{N/2}$ possible subsets of its element and store them in an array of length $2^{N/2}$.
- Sort the arrays, it require 0 ($2^{N/2}N$.)

## 5.4. Graph Coloring

### Concept

For a given graph, find the smallest number of colors that need to be assigned to the graph's vertices so that no two adjacent vertices are assigned to same color.

Given an undirected graph G (v, E) where V- set of vertices and E- set of edges,it is required to find out an assignment of colors to vertices, such that no 2vertices which are connected by an edge would get the same color.

### 5.4.1. Procedure for Graph Coloring

- The basic idea behind the solution is that once a vertex is assigned a color then all the vertices which are connected to that are refrained from using the same color.
- We have some set of color C, then initially all the color are available to all the vertices.
- We start assigning colors to the vertices; the number of available colors to the remaining vertices would also start reducing depending on the existence of edges between vertices.

The deterministic solution to the graph coloring problem uses this observation to assign colors to the vertices.

### Process of Assigning Color to Vertices

- We are given graph G = (V, E) and set of colors C = ($C_1$, $C_2$, $C_3$, $C_4$, $C_n$)
- Sort the vertices in non decreasing order of their node degree.
- Build a list of available colors to each vertex. Initially all colors are available to all vertices.
- Now select the first vertex from the set of sorted vertices and for the selected vertex assign the first available color so that color is not assigned to its adjacent vertices.
- For example, the first vertex $V_1$ can be assigned color $C_1$, then all the vertices which are connected to $V_1$ cannot use $C_1$. So remove $C_1$ from available colors for all vertices which are connected to $V_1$.
- Repeat step 4 till no vertex remains unassigned.

### Example for Graph Coloring

### Example 1

Consider the graph shown below whose adjacency list is also shown by its side

| Vertex | Adjacency vertex |
|--------|------------------|
| 1 | 2, 3 |
| 2 | 1, 3, 5 |
| 3 | 1,2,4,5 |
| 4 | 3, 5 |
| 5 | 2, 3, 4 |

Let the set of available -colors

C = {Red, Green, Blue, Yellow)

### Assign Color to All Vertices

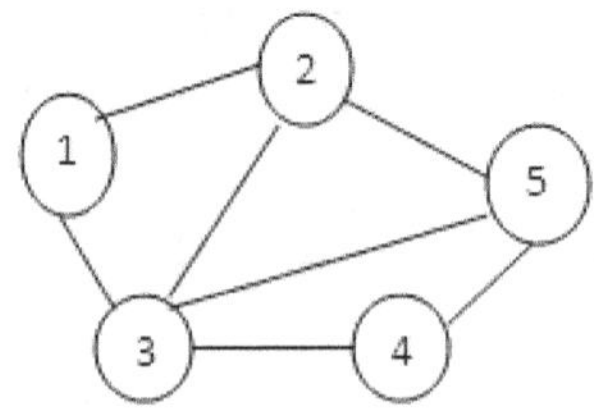

Sort all the vertices in decreasing order of their node degrees.

{V3, V2, V5, V1, V4}

Now, we start with V3 and assign the first color "Red" to it, them all 'its adjacent vertices $V_2, V_5, V_1$ and $V_4$ cannot use "Red".

So we can construct a table

| Vertex | Red | Green | Blue | Yellow |
|--------|-----|-------|------|--------|
| V3 | √ | | | |
| V2 | X | | | |
| V5 | X | | | |
| V1 | X | | | |
| V4 | X | | | |

where

√ Indicates vertex is assigned that color.

x indicates vertex cannot be assigned that color.

- Empty indicates that color is available.
- The next vertex"$V_2$" cannot use "Red" color. So the next color Green is assigned to vertex $V_2$. The adjacent vertices $V_1, V_3, V_5$ cannot use "Green" color.

| Vertex | Red | Green | Blue | Yellow |
|--------|-----|-------|------|--------|
| V3 | √ | X | | |
| V2 | X | √ | | |
| V5 | X | X | | |
| V1 | X | X | | |
| V4 | X | | | |

- The next vertex $V_5$ cannot use Red & Green color. The next available color "Blue" is assigned to vertex $V_1$. Its adjacent vertices are 2, 3 cannot use "Blue" color.

| Vertex | Red | Green | Blue | Yellow |
|--------|-----|-------|------|--------|
| V3 | √ | X | X | |
| V2 | X | √ | X | |
| V5 | X | X | √ | |
| V1 | X | X | X | |
| V4 | X | | X | |

- The next vertex $V_1$ can be assigned with any one of the color blue or yellow.

  So $V_1$ can be assigned with 6'Blue"color.

- The next vertex $V_4$ can be assigned with any one of the color green or yellow. So $V_4$ can be assigned with green color.

| Vertex | Red | Green | Blue | Yellow |
|--------|-----|-------|------|--------|
| V3 | √ | X | X | |
| V2 | X | √ | X | |
| V5 | X | X | √ | |
| V1 | X | X | √ | |
| V4 | X | √ | X | |

So the chromatic number=3

## Example 2: Consider the Following Graph

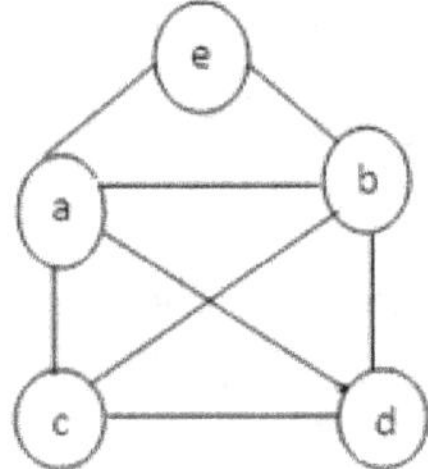


Let the set of available colors

c = {color 1, color 2, color 3, color 4)

Assign colors to all the vertices

- Sort all the vertices in decreasing order of their node degrees.

  {c, b,c,e,d}

- Now we start with 'a' and assign the first color 'color 1' to it then all its adjacent vertices b, c, e cannot use 'color1'

So we can construct a table.

| vertex | color 1 | color 2 | color 3 | color 4 |
|--------|---------|---------|---------|---------|
| a | √ | | | |
| b | X | | | |
| c | X | | | |
| d | | | | |
| e | X | | | |

- The next vertex 'b' cannot use "color 1" so the next color, color 2 is assigned to 'b', its adjacent vertices are 'a',' e',' c' cannot use 'color 2'.

| Vertex | color 1 | color 2 | color 3 | color 4 |
|--------|---------|---------|---------|---------|
| a | √ | X | | |
| b | X | √ | | |
| c | X | X | | |
| d | | | | |
| e | X | X | | |

- The next vertex c cannot use color 1 & color 2. The next available color, color 3 is assigned to ' c '. Its adjacent vertices 'a','d' &' b' cannot use color 3.

| Vertex | color 1 | color 2 | color 3 | color 4 |
|--------|---------|---------|---------|---------|
| a | √ | X | X | |
| b | X | √ | X | |
| c | X | X | √ | |
| d | | | X | |
| e | X | X | | |

- The next vertex d cannot use color 3 .it can be assigned with color 1 or color 2. So d is assigned with color 1.

| Vertex | color 1 | color 2 | color 3 | color 4 |
|--------|---------|---------|---------|---------|
| a | √ | X | X | |
| b | X | √ | X | |
| c | X | X | √ | |
| d | √ | | X | |
| e | X | X | | |

- The next vertex e cannot use color 1 & color 2. The next available color, color 3 is assigned to ' e '. Its adjacent vertices 'a','d' &' b' cannot use color 3.

| Vertex | color 1 | color 2 | color 3 | color 4 |
|--------|---------|---------|---------|---------|
| a | √ | X | X | |
| b | X | √ | X | |
| c | X | X | √ | |
| d | √ | | X | |
| e | X | X | √ | |

So the chromatic number=3

### Chromatic Number

The chromatic number of a graph G is the smallest number of colors needed to color the vertices of G so that no two adjacent vertices share the same color.

### Algorithm for Graph Coloring

void mcoloring (k)

//This algorithm using the recursive backtracking schema.

// The graph is represented by its adjacency

//MatrixG[1: n, l: n]

// k is the index of the next vertex to color

{

repeat

{

// Generate all legal assignment for x[k]

nextvalue (k)          //assign to x[k] a legal color

if(x[k]= =0)          //no new color possible

return;

if(k==n)          at most m color have been used

Output (x [1: n];          to color the n vertices.

else

mcoloring (k+1);

} until (false);

}

void  nextvalue (k)

//x[1],...x[k+1] have been assigned integer values is the range [1, m], such that

//adjacent vertices have district integers.

//A value for x [k] is determined in the range [0, m]

// x [k] is assigned the next highest numbered color

repeat

{

x [k] = (x [k +1]) mod (m+1); // next highest color.

if(x [k] = =0)                    // All color have been used.

return;

for(j =1; j <n; j++)

{

//check if this color is

// distinct from adjacent colors.

if((G[k][j]≠0)&&(x[k]==x[j]))

break;

}

if(j = = n+1) // new color found

return;

} until (false); // otherwise try to find another color

}

***Complexity for Graph Coloring***

***Computing Time of m Coloring***

Time required for next value algorithm=O(mn)

Time required for m coloring algorithm

$$= \sum_{i=1}^{n} m^i n$$

$$= \frac{n (m^{n+1} - 2)}{(m - 1)}$$

$$= O (n m^n)$$

## 5.5. Hamiltonian Cycle Problem

### *Concept*

Let G = (V. E) be a connected graph with n vertices. A Hamiltonian cycle is a round trip path along n edges of G that visits every vertex once and returns to its starting position.

In other words if a Hamiltonian cycle begins at some vertex $V_1$ ∈G and the vertices of G are visited is the order $V_1$, $V_2$, . . ..$V_{n+1}$, then the edges ($V_1$, $V_{i+1}$ ) are in E, 1≤ i ≤ n and the $V_i$ are distinct except for $V_1$ and $V_{n+1}$ which are equal.

### *Procedure for Hamiltonian Cycles*

- The graph may be directed or undirected.
- The graph is stored as an adjacency matrix G [1: n, 1: n].
- If x[k] =0, then no vertex has been assigned to x[k].
- X[1: k-1] is a path of k-1 distinct vertices.
- All cycles begins at node 1.
- During the execution x[k] is assigned to the next highest numbered vertex which does not already appear in x[1: k-1] and is connected by an edge x[k-1], otherwise x[k] assigned to zero.
- If k = n, then x[k] is connected to x[i].

### *Example 1*

Find the Hamiltonian cycle for the following graph

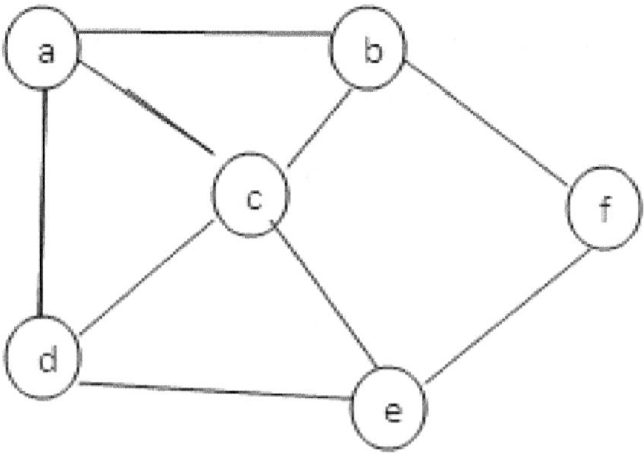

Find Hamiltonian cycle for the following graph.

- We make vertex a be the root of the state space tree.
- The adjacent vertices for 'a' are b, c & d.
- We select vertex b. It proceeds b to c, then to d, then to e and finally to f, which leads to dead end.
- The algorithm backtracks from f to e, then to d and then to c then to b and it finds another alternative solution.
- Now the algorithm proceeds b to f, then to e then to c, then to d, then to e finally it reaches to start vertex.

***Algorithm for Hamiltonian Cycle***

***Void Hamiltonian (k)***

// This algorithm uses the recursive formulation of backtracking

//It finds all the Hamiltonian cycles of a graph

// The graph is stored as adjacency matrix G [1:n,1:n]

//All cycles begins at node 1.

{

repeat

   { // Generate values for x [k]

     nextvalue (k); // Assign legal value k

     if (x [k] = = 0)

       return;

     if( k = = n) //The last vertex and print all the vertices.

   outputs (x [1: n]);

    else

       Hamiltonian (k+l);

} Until (false);

}

Algorithm for finding next vertex in the Hamiltonian cycle.

### *void next value (k)*

//x [1: k-1] is a path of k-1 distinct vertices

//If x[k] = 0, then no vertex has been assigned to x[k].

// After execution x[k] is assigned to the next highest numbered vertex, which does not

  appear in x [1: k-1] and is connected by an edge to x[k-1].

// Otherwise x[k]= 0

//if k= n, then x[k] is connected to x[1]

 repeat

{

x [k] (x [k]+ 1) mod (n+ 1); // next vertex

if(x[k]==0)

return;

if(G [x[k-1],x[k]J= = 0)

{ //is there an edge

for(j=1;j <=k-1;j++)

if(x[j]= = x[k])

//If tree, then the vertex is distinct

{

if((k < n)||((k = = n) && G[x [n] [x [1]]))

 return;

}

}

}

### *Complexity for Hamiltonian Cycle*

### *Time Complexity*

Number of edges in the graph=n

Cost of one edge=c

Total cost for all edges in the graph=cn

$$=O(n)$$

## 5.6. 0/1 Knapsack Problem

### *Concept*

The solution to the problem has the form $\{x_1, x_2, ..., x_n\}$ where $x_i = 1$ , $i^{th}$ item is placed in the knapsack, otherwise $x_i = 0$.

Each item has both a weight $w_i$ and a profit $p_i$.

The goal is to maximize the total profit

$$\sum_{i=1}^{n} p_i x_i$$

Subject to the knapsack capacity constraint

$$\sum_{i=1}^{n} w_i x_i \leq m \text{ and } 0 \leq x_i \leq 1$$

### *General Procedure for 0/1 Knapsack Problem*

- Arrange all the items in descending order of profit /weight ratio.
- A partial solution to the problem is one in which only the first k items have been considered.
- The solution has the form

$S_K = \{x_1, x_2, ..., x_k\}$ where I <k<n

The partial solution $S_k$ is feasible if and only if

$$\sum_{i=1}^{k} w_i x_i \leq m$$

If $S_k$ is feasible, the total profit of any solution containing $S_k$ is bounded by

$$\sum_{i=1}^{k} p_i x_i + \sum_{i=k+1} p_i x_i$$

The solution generated by the greedy method has all $x_i$'s equal to zero or one.

We partition the solution space into 2 subspaces one is $x_i=0$ and the other $x_i=1$

### *Example for 0/1Knapsack*

Find the optimal solution for the following items using 0/1 knapsack problem.

n=4, w=16

| Item | Profit | Weight | Profit/Weight |
|------|--------|--------|---------------|
| (i) | $(p_i)$ | (wi) | $p_i/w_i$ |
| 1 | $40 | 2 | 20 |
| 2 | $30 | 5 | 6 |
| 3 | $50 | 10 | 5 |
| 4 | $10 | 5 | 2 |

### *Calculation for Root Node i.e., Node 1*

a. Profit = 0

Weight 0

b. bound = profit + P1 + P2 + (w-7) * $P_3/w_3$

= 0+40+30+(16 - 7) x 50/10

c. It is promising node because its weight=0<w<16 and its bound 115>0

so node 1 is expanded..

### *Calculation for 2nd Node*

Item 1 with profit  $40 and weight 2 is included.

(a)　Max profit = $40

　　　Weight =2

(b)　Bound　　= Profit + $P_2$ + (w - 7) x $P_3/W_3$

　　　　　　=$40 + $30 + 9x 50/10

　　　　　　=$ 115.

(c)　Node 2 is promising node, because its weight is 2 <w ≤ 16 and its bound $115 > $ 40. So the node 2 is expanded.

## Calculation for Node 3

Item 2 with profit $30 and weight 5 is included.

(a)  Max profit = $30 + $40

Weight =5+2

(b)  bound     = profit + (w - 7) X P3/W3

=$ 70+9x50/10

=$115

(c)  It is also promising node because its weight 0 <w < 16 and bound 115 >70.

so it is expanded.

## Calculation for Node 4

Item 3 with profit 50 and weight 10 is included.

(a)  Max profit = $30 +$40 + $50= 120

Weight = 5 +2 + 10

(b)  bound = 120

(c)  It is non promising node because its weight 17> 16 and its bound 115 < 120

So, the node 4 is not expanded.

## Calculation for Node 5

Item 3 with profit $50 and weight -10 is excluded.

(a) Profit = $ 40+ $30

Weight = 7

(b) bound     = profit + (16— 7) x 10/5

= 70+9x10/5   =88

(c) Node 5 is promising node because its weight < 16 & profit 88<70

so it is expanded.

## Calculation for Node 6

Item 4 with profit 10 and weight is included.

(a)  Profit =$40+$30+$10

Weight = 12

(b)  bound = profit = 80

(c)  Node 6 is non promising node, its upper bound 80 = 80 it cannot be expanded.

### Calculation for Node 7

Item 3 and 4 is not included.

(a)   Profit = $40 + $ 30

    Weight = 7

(b)   bound = 70

(c)   It is also non promising node because its profit = bound.

### Calculation for Node 8

Item 2 is not included.

(a)   Profit = 40

    Weight =2

(b)   bound==$40+$50+(16—12)X10 / 5

       = $40 + $50 + $8

       =$98

(c)   It is also promising node, its max profit <bound

### Calculation for Node 9

Item 3 with profit 50 and weight 10 is included.

(a) Profit =$40+$5090

   Weight =2+10=12

(b) bound   = profit+(I6—12)x10 / 5

       = 90+4 x 10 / 5

       = 98

(c) It is promising node because profit <98 so it is expanded.

### Calculation for Node 10

Item 4 with profit 10 and weight 5 is included.

(a)   Profit = $40+$50+$10

    Weight=2+5+10

(b)   bound=100

(c)   It is also non promising node because profit = bound, so it is not expanded.

## Calculation for Node 11

Item 4 is not included

(a)Profit= $40+$50

　　Weight=2+10= 12

(b) Bound =90

　(c) It is non promising node, it is not expended

## Calculation for Node 12

Item 1 with $40 and weight 2 is not included. At this point maximum profit is

$90.

(a) Profit = 0

　　Weight = 0

(b) Bound　 = Profit + P2 + P4 + (16 — 15) *

　　　　　　= 0+50+30+2

　　　　　　=82

(c) It is non-promising node, bound> profit so it is not expanded.

F → Not feasible

N →Not Optimal

B →Cannot lead to best solution

## Algorithm for 0/1 Knapsack Problem

```
void BKnap (k, cp,cw)
// m is the size of the knapsack
// n is the number of weights and profits
// w[ ]and p[ ] are the weights and profits
// P[i] /w[il>=P[i+l]/w[i+1]
// fw is the final weight of knapsack
// fp is the final maximum profit
// x[k]=0, if w [k] is not in the knapsack else x[k] = 1.
{// Generate left child
```

```
  if(Cw+w[k]<m)
  {
    y[k]=1;
    if(k<n)
Bknap (k+1, Cp + P [k], Cw + w[k]);
if((Cp + P [k] > fp) and (CK = = n))
{
fpCp+P[kl;
f=C+w[k];
for(j=l:j <=k;j++)
x[j]=y[j];
}
}
//Generate right child
if (Bound (CP,Cw, k)> P)
{
     y[k]=0;
if(k<n)
BKnap (k+1, Cp, Cw);
if((Cp> f)&&(K==n))
{
fp=Cp;
fw=Cw:
for (j=1;j <= k;j++)
x[j]=y[j];
}
}
}
```

***Algorithm for Bound Function***

**void Bound (C$_p$, C$_w$, k)**

//C$_p$, is the current profit total

//C$_w$ is current weight total

//K is the index of last removed item

//m is the knapsack size

{

b=C$_p$;

c=C$_w$;

for (i=K+1 ; i<=n ; i++)

{

C=C+w[i];

if(C <m)

b =b + P [iJ;

else

return (b + (1-(c-rn) / w[i])) * P [i] ;

}

return b;

}

## *Complexity for 0/1 Knapsack Problem*

- All the item arc arranged in sorted order
- So it requires O(n) comparison.

# TWO MARK QUESTIONS & ANSWERS

**1. *State if backtracking always produces optimal solution? (May/June '08)***

Yes, the idea of the backtracking can be further enhanced by evaluating the quality of partially constructed solution.

**2. *How will you construct an optimal binary search, tree? (May/Julie '06)***

- A binary search tree is one of the most important data structure in computer since
- One of its principle application to implement a dictionary, a set of elements with the operation of searching, insertion and deletion.
- If probabilities of searching elements in a set are known as optimal binary search tree.
- It requires only average number of comparisons.

*Example*

4 Keys A, B. C & D to be searched with possibilities 0.1, 0.2, 0.3 &0.4 respectively.

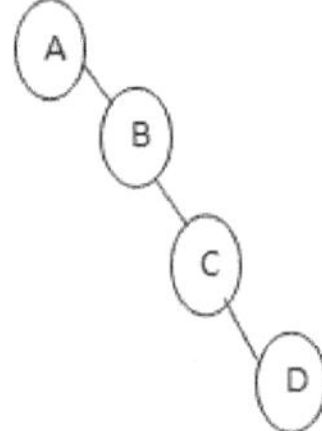

**3. *Define backtracking (May/Julie '06)***

It is a kind of solving problem by trial and error. We make sure that we never try the same thing twice; we also make sure that if the problem is finite, and we will eventually try all possibilities.

Backtracking problem require that all the solutions satisfy the complex set of constraints.

**4. *What is Hamiltonian cycle in an undirected graph? (May/June '06)***

A Hamiltonian cycle is round trip along n edges of 0 that visits every vertex once and returns to its starting position.

If a Hamiltonian cycle begins at some vertex V1 ϵ G and the vertices of G are visited in the order V1, V2. V+1, then the edges (V1, V1+1) are in E, I <i <n and the V1 are distinct except for Vi.

## 5. *What is meant by slate space tree? (No v/ Dec '06,)*

Backtracking algorithm determine problem solutions by systematically searching the solution space for the given problem instance. This search is facilitated _sing a tree organization by the solution space.

- Each node in the tree defines a problem state.
- All path from root to other node define the state space of the problem.
- V Solution states are those problem states s for which the path from the root to s defines a tuple in the solution space.
- "F Answer state are those solution state s for which the path from the root to s defines a tuple that is a member of the set of solutions.

## 6. *Explain the term solution state, Answer state, E-node and dead node*

### *Solution State*

The problem state S for which the path from the root to S define a tuple in the solution space.

Answer state -Leaf node which correspond to an element in the set of solution

E-node -A node being expanded.

Dead Node -A node expanded completely, not to be expanded, further.

## 7. *What type of constraints used in backtracking problem?*

Backtracking problem require that all the solution satisfy a cornplex set of constraints.

Two types of constraints are

1. Implicit constraint
2. Explicit constraint

### *Implicit Constraint*

The implicit constraints are rule that determine which solution space of I satisfy the criterion function. The implicit constraint describe the way in which the xi relate to each other.

### *Explicit Constraint*

Explicit constraints are rule that restrict each x to take on values from a i— set.

$x_i >= 0$ $S_1 = \{$ All non negative real numbers)

$x_i = 0$ (or) $x_, = 1$, $S_1 = \{0, 1\}$

### 8. What is the time complexity for backtracking algorithm?

There are 4 factors, that determine the time required by a backtracking algorithm.

- The time to generate the next XK ie solution node.
- The number of XK (solution node) satisfying the explicit constraints.
- The time for the bounding function BK.
- The number of solution nodes generated

Number of nodes in the solution space = n!

Worst case time complexity = 0 (P (n) n!)

Where P — probability of successful search.

### 9. Define 8 Queens Problem

The problem is to place 8 queens on an 8 by 8 chess board, so that no 2 queens attack each other being in the same row (or) in the same column or in the diagnol.

### 10. How to identify whether the 2 Queens on the same diagonal

To identify whether the 2 Queens on the same diagonal it must satisfy the following conditions.

1. Every element on the same diagonal that runs from upper left to the lower right have same (row ,column) value.
2. Also every element on the same diagonal that goes from the upper right to lower left have the same (row + column) value.

### 11. What is the time complexity of 8 Queens Problem?

- In 8 x 8 chess board, there are (64k) possible ways to place 8 queens.
- Initially we can select any one of n values for queen 1.
- Next, we can select any one of n -1 values for queen 2 and so on.
- Finally we can select one remaining values for queen 8.
- It tests 8! Configurations i.e., [ 40320]

### 12. What is meant by sum of subset problem?

We are given a distinct positive numbers (usually called weights) and we desire to find all combination of these numbers, whose sums are 'm'. This is called the sum of subsets problem.

### 13. How to identify bounded node in sum of subset problem

The bounded node can be identified with the following condition

BK(X1,X2,........XK) = tree

iff $\sum$ wixi (i=1 to k) + $\sum$wixi$\geq$m (i=k+1 to n)

### 14. What is the time complexity of sum of subs et problem ?

- The algorithm splits arbitrarily N elements into 2 sets of N/2 each.
- For each of these 2 sets, it calculates sum of all 22 possible subsets of its element and store them in an array of length 22.
- Sort the array, it require 0 (2 N) comparisons.

### 15. What is meant by graph coloring?

For a given graph, find the smallest number of colors, that need to be assignc -'to the graphs, vertices, so that no 2 adjacent vertices are assigned the same color.

### 16. Define Chromatic number?

The chromatic number of a graph 0 is the smallest number of color color the verities of G, so that no 2 adjacent vertices share the same color.

### 17. What is the time complexity for graph coloring?

Time required for next value algorithm = 0 (m.n)

Time required for m coloring algorithm=$\sum$ m^i n (for i-1 to n)

$$=n(m^n+1 -2)/(m-1)$$

$$=0(n\ m^n).$$

### 18. Define Hamiltonian cycle?

Let G=(V,E) be a connected graph with n vertices. A Hamiltonian cycle is a round trip path along n edges of AG that visits every other vertex once and returns to the starting position.

### 19. What is the time complexity for Hamiltonian Cycle?

Number of edges in the graph = n

Cost of one edge = c

Total cost for all edges in the graph $\quad$ = n x c

$$= 0(n)$$

### 20. Explain 0/1 knapsack problem

The solution to the problem has the from {x1, x2, ..... xn} where xi is one ith  item is placed in the knapsack, otherwise xi= 0.

The goal is to maximize the total profit : $\sum$ Pi Xi (for i-1 to n)

Subject to the knapsack capacity constraint

$$\sum \text{wixi} < m \ \& \ 0 \leq \text{xi} \leq 1$$

### 21. Differentiate b/w promising and non promising node on 0/1 knapsack problem

| Promising Node | Non promising node |
|---|---|
| • Its weightless than the capacity of knapsack<br>• Upper bound>max profit.<br>• The node can be expanded further. | • Its weight is greater than knapsack capacity.<br>• Upper bound<max profit.<br>• The node cannot be expanded further. |